CRITICAL THINKING:

The Claim Shredder Method

FARUK RAHMANOVIC

Copyright © 2021 by Faruk Rahmanovic
All rights reserved

Editors:
Michael Owens, M.Ed.
Steven Starke, Ph.D.
Nicholas Dovellos, Ph.D.

Designer:
Kristen Thorley

For Majda and Sufian

Table of Contents

INTRODUCTION

If you take a programming class and read a book on programming, you expect to be able to program at the end of it. If you take a math class and read a book about mathematics, you expect to be able to do that kind of math at the end of it – or at least do it better than when you started. This is a book on critical thinking. So, by the end of it, you should expect to be a critical thinker.

So, what exactly is critical thinking?

Critical thinking is an intellectual skill used to examine ideas, and to do so in a way that gives us a clear, concise, transparent, and meaningful conclusion about whether the idea works, or whether it is garbage.

Why is critical thinking important? Or, if you prefer, *why should you spend both the money to buy the book, the time to read and understand it, and then the effort to use this skill?*

Let's use an example I like to give to my students on day 1 of teaching a class on critical thinking (going through this book is the equivalent of taking that class):

You should care about this class, and put in the right kind of effort, because this is the most important class you can take.

That is a very big claim, especially for people that are not into philosophy and are commonly only there for a general education requirement. How can I defend that idea?

Philosophy (and critical thinking in particular) is all about how to think; how to properly use your reason to understand the world around you and to navigate your way through it. Every field of interest and study ever invented (yes, even Interpretive Dance), is based on thinking and the use of reason. That means that, if you can learn how to think and use your reason better, you can be better at every single thing you do. Every part of your life - academic, professional, personal, etc. can be made better if you understand critical thinking. Therefore, this one skill can have positive effects on everything you do for the rest of your life. Is there another skill you could pursue that makes a claim like that? No. Every other skill gives you ideas and practices you can use in some particular field. Only philosophy makes this kind of claim for every aspect of your life.

Critical thinking allows you to use reason better. Therefore, if you put in the effort and properly understand and use this skill, it will help you make better decisions for anything you do, for the rest of your life. This is why a book like this represents the most important skill you can learn; because it teaches you a single skill that translates into making meaningfully better decisions everywhere and all the time - no matter the context. So, the reason why you should invest money, time, and effort into this skill is because this skill will help you with every other issue you face and interest you have.

The goal of this book is to teach you critical thinking skills, from the ground up. By the end of this book, you will be able to understand why each part of the process is important, and how to best use it for your own needs.

How was this text developed?

When I started teaching philosophy, I ran into a bit of a problem: all the critical thinking textbooks I examined lacked a clear methodology for critical thinking. They told the reader to "think harder" but failed to explain what exactly that means. They told the reader to get the context, without explaining how to do so, or how to recognize that they don't have enough context. There was a lot of jargon, but it didn't really contribute to the understanding of the skill for students.

On top of that, I found out that most students lacked critical thinking skills; the few students who did have a grasp on it still did not have a systematic way of using that skill. As a result, they spent a lot more time and effort in making it work than was necessary. Fact of the matter is, when a skill is difficult, we tend to skip using it, unless we absolutely have to. If you **can** cook, but it's very difficult and time-consuming, then you likely don't cook unless you have no other choice. Find an expert at cooking, and you'll find someone who cooks for fun - because the skill is second nature to them.

This was equally true everywhere I went: high schools, community colleges, major 4-year institutions, even the exclusive Honors Colleges filled with pre-med students. That means that this is not an issue of "quality" of your high school or college, but a general issue we all face. For example, the biggest hurdle on the MCAT for many students is not the science part, but the critical thinking portion. That's because, unlike the science part - for which they spent years preparing - they have had no meaningful training in critical thinking. To make sure that my students were getting the best education I could provide, I started writing my own content for them.

Around the same time, I had the opportunity to talk to an expert on cybersecurity and a CISO (chief information security officer) for a Fortune 500 company. When I explained the method I had developed for critical thinking, they were impressed enough to invite me to present it to their team as a better way of doing cybersecurity analysis. Now, a disclaimer: I know nothing about cybersecurity; I cannot code my way out of a wet paper bag. That means that all I could present was philosophy and critical thinking. All I could offer was a way to think better, in a clear, concise, and transparent way - in order to solve **any problem, in any field**. The only thing related to cybersecurity in my presentation was the case study and a few examples. But the presentation could be exactly the same for any field at all.

The presentation was a hit, and I was invited to present again at a national conference - where the *Claim Shredder Method* was adopted as standard procedure for the cybersecurity analysts. Following that, I presented it to an international community of cybersecurity analysts, who also adopted it. And again, I don't know the first thing about cybersecurity. The entire presentation was nothing more than content I had developed for my critical thinking courses.

Ultimately, this book is the long form of that presentation. It walks you through all the key components of critical thinking - making sure you understand not only **what** to do, but **why** you're doing it. Additionally, the *Claim Shredder Method* avoids the problems of the other critical thinking textbooks, by giving you a very clear process to follow. This gives you a "how-to" component to the course. As I had started teaching, I also noticed that many of my students viewed philosophy and critical thinking as something strictly Western - a product of Europe in the last few hundred years. Given my extensive academic background in non-Western culture and philosophy, and my personal experiences (Sarajevo has been a melting pot of East and West for the last 600 years), it seemed rather strange that the use of reason to comprehend and solve problems should be viewed as somehow a feature of only one small part of the world.

Part of the problem, of course, was that most people are simply not exposed to non-Western thinkers and cultures in their own education. In order to pack in as much educational content as I could, I made sure that I presented a multicultural selection of content. In response, I found that my students engaged more effectively when given a wider variety of ideas and examples to draw from. Additionally, seeing that the same intellectual issues we were dealing with today had been explored 4,000 years ago in India, 3,000 years ago in China, 1,000 years ago in the Middle East, etc. gave my students an appreciation for the universal nature of the problems we face as human beings, the kinds of intellectual similarities that can be found across cultural differences, and a very diverse and interesting range of solutions developed by very different peoples and cultures around the world, across history. For that reason, and because certain ideas have been much better communicated by non-Western thinkers, you will find that this book uses a multicultural approach to critical thinking, whenever that is the best way to explore an idea.

Finally, a common complaint of many students taking philosophy classes can be summed up as, *when is something like this ever going to be useful?* I thought that was a fair point: if philosophy is taught only in the abstract, it can be difficult to understand its value. So, I made sure that my own approach was focused on making the content as practical as possible. The point became to grasp how very abstract ideas have a very real impact on the lives of ordinary people. One of the best ways I found to get this point across was to demonstrate the interdisciplinary value of abstract ideas; to show how an abstract philosophical idea plays out in various academic and professional fields, and how it actually affects people in their private lives - from their families to romantic relationships. While I cannot tailor the examples of this book to each and every reader (like I do for my students) you will find that this book uses examples from across a number of disciplines - and hopefully at least a few that are of interest to you. That way, the content is more likely to stick, which means that the ideas presented here are more likely to become part of your daily routine.

How does this Book Work?

The book is divided up into four parts.

In the first part, we look at the ideas of emotion and reason, the ways in which emotion can often cloud our judgment, and ways to remain rational when faced with ideas and issues that might otherwise push us into fits of emotion. This is an important part of critical thinking, because emotional outbursts are the opposite of critical thinking.

In the second part, we look at claims, problems, and some crucial points about how to deal with ideas. In this section, you will learn how arguments are constructed - so that you can start to take them apart. You will also learn the kinds of problems that usually sneak their way into our ideas and ruin them.

In the third part, we will look at the ideas of context - the key feature of critical thinking. When the context is missing, you can't agree or disagree with anything that is said, because you have no idea what is being said. You will learn what questions to ask, in what order, and why. You will also learn what kinds of answers do and don't work, and how to take apart ideas to see all the moving parts inside. This tells us whether the idea can be broken, and how.

Finally, in the fourth part, we put everything together into that neat little package called the *Claim Shredder Method*. In this section, you will learn the step-by-step process for dealing with any claim you might come across. As part of that process, we will also look at a detailed process of taking apart a famous claim in a case study and see exactly how the *Claim Shredder Method* actually works in practice. With a flowchart to visually guide you through the process, you will be just as capable of critical thinking in any area of your own life and interests, with similarly effective results.

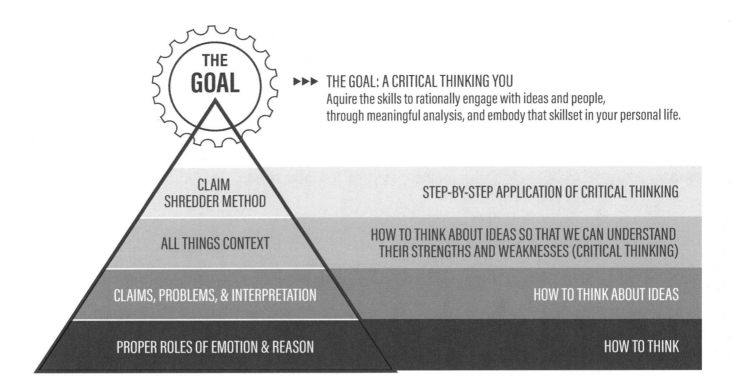

THE GOAL ▶▶▶ THE GOAL: A CRITICAL THINKING YOU
Aquire the skills to rationally engage with ideas and people, through meaningful analysis, and embody that skillset in your personal life.

CLAIM SHREDDER METHOD	STEP-BY-STEP APPLICATION OF CRITICAL THINKING
ALL THINGS CONTEXT	HOW TO THINK ABOUT IDEAS SO THAT WE CAN UNDERSTAND THEIR STRENGTHS AND WEAKNESSES (CRITICAL THINKING)
CLAIMS, PROBLEMS, & INTERPRETATION	HOW TO THINK ABOUT IDEAS
PROPER ROLES OF EMOTION & REASON	HOW TO THINK

What This Book Does Not Do:

With a name like *Claim Shredder Method*, you might think this book is geared towards being argumentative, aggressive, and designed to rip ideas to shreds. That is not the case. Well, it is, but there's much more to it.

First, the *Claim Shredder Method* is not a tool of sophistry (arguing for the sake of "winning," with no regard for the truth) - aka *Trolling*. Imagine a paper shredder: it is a tool that uses a specific kind of weakness of what you put into it, to tear it apart. Paper is the kind of thing that has this specific kind of weakness. As a result, if you put paper into a paper shredder, it gets shredded - the shredder takes advantage of the weakness, and destroys the object.

But, imagine what happens if you put a steel plate into the paper shredder. The steel plate will be just fine. That is not because the shredder did not do its job. Instead, it is because the steel plate does not have the kind of weakness that can be taken advantage of by the shredder. This is the big idea: you want to be able to identify bad claims, and take them apart. You don't want to accidentally reject good claims. The fact that you can "win" a debate is meaningless if you still believe a bad claim.

Second, despite the possibly argumentative conclusions we might reach by disagreeing with a claim, the *Claim Shredder Method* is not an aggressive approach that seeks to "win" over others (more on that in Chapter 2). Instead, the *Claim Shredder Method* is much more of a cooperative effort to **explore** ideas, in order to determine whether they work or not. We want this cooperation, because it is much easier when the people bringing the idea are working with us, instead of against us. If you meaningfully engage with people and ideas, and try to understand them the best you can, they tend to work with you, not against you. Additionally, when we are working together (instead of against each other), it is far easier for both sides to acknowledge when their ideas are broken.

Finally, if we want to find the truth - as best we can - then we must be ready to accept that our **own ideas might be wrong**. For this reason, as we use the *Claim Shredder Method*, we are not only checking whether the ideas of other people work; we are simultaneously checking whether our own ideas on that topic are functional. Personally, I have never been interested in holding onto my ideas; I would much rather discover that I was wrong and change my position, than keep on believing in something that is actually wrong. Truth, even painful truth, has some kind of value as it informs our ideas about the world. False ideas may be comfortable, but all they can do is trick us into believing that we understand what is going on - right up until we walk off a cliff.

Some Study Suggestions:

Since you are already here, putting in time, effort, and resources, you might as well get the most out of this book. The following several suggestions for how to approach this text will help you get the most out of it.

One of the most common points I tell my students is that the most effective reading happens when we **focus on understanding the text, instead of trying to be "right."** What does that mean? The first time you read a text, you should not be concerned about whether the author is right or wrong. Instead, you should focus on understanding what they are trying to communicate to you. Once you understand that, then you can go back and see whether they are right or wrong about their ideas.

I am sure that you will read some things in this text that will cause you to want to argue. That's fine. However, before you start arguing, take a minute to read (or re-read) the entire chapter. Make sure you understand what is happening, and then - if you still disagree - argue against it. By the way, the same goes with agreeing with the book. This is important: agreeing with an idea without understanding it is just as bad as disagreeing with it. If you miss the point that was being made, you can end up agreeing with (or arguing against) things that are not actually there. It happens to all of us, so consider this a useful reminder.

Second, the best way of learning is by relating the content to your own experiences. As you read along, ask yourself if you have ever seen this sort of an issue, or have been in this kind of a situation, etc. Take a moment to take a break from the reading, and think about how the ideas relate to you, personally. If you do that, the ideas will stick much better, and you will be able to use them much easier.

Better yet, try to apply the lessons you have learned in your daily interactions - whether with people or ideas. See how effective the ideas really are, firsthand. We are not in the habit of taking time to really think, which is understandable, given the very fast pace of our lives and the sheer quantity of information that is thrown at us daily. That means that, truly embodying critical thinking requires us to replace our current default behaviors with new ones. No amount of knowledge will help with this; it is just something you have to **do** often enough that you develop a new default reflex for interacting with ideas. The sooner you start, the sooner you will get better at it.

Third, you will notice that we will use a decent amount of interesting or strange terminology throughout the text. I have tried to eliminate as much jargon as possible, but some terms and ideas are just the sort of thing we have to deal with. As soon as you are not positive that you could define the word to someone else, and do so clearly, you should stop reading and look up the definition. This is critical: if you're not sure about the meaning of a word, you will not be able to fully understand the ideas. And because the entire course builds on itself, that means that missing parts of earlier ideas will lead you to have a weaker understanding of later ideas. On top of that, looking up unfamiliar words will expand your vocabulary - which is always a positive. If you have a voice activated phone, you can just yell at your phone to define the word for you, without having to disrupt your reading.

I wish you all the best of luck and happy critical thinking!

Faruk Rahmanovic, Ph.D.

CHAPTER 1

THINKING CLEARLY

Welcome to the first section! Over the next three chapters, we will take a look at reason, emotion, and how the two do and don't work for proper ways of thinking - and why. This will give us the basic groundwork for critical thinking. Additionally, you should be able to recognize all these features in your own behaviors, confirm their truth from your own experiences, and begin to work on developing better critical thinking habits by understanding yourself.

You might think that critical thinking is the kind of thing we all do, at least decently. After all, if the definition we gave a moment ago is correct, then we really need critical thinking to make anything work - from our personal lives to society. But, as seems to be the case with common sense, it is not nearly as common as we think it is.

There is a difference between thinking, and critical thinking. Thinking is the process by which we examine and evaluate ideas. We do it all day, every day - and if (as science suggests) your dreams are a way for your brain to process information, then you literally do it in your sleep! What makes critical thinking different is the kind of approach we take to thinking, so that we can get a clear, concise, transparent, and meaningful conclusion about whether the idea works, or whether it is garbage.

So, what's the difference?

Critical thinking is the approach that tries to strip off the various confusing influences[1] in our thinking, leaving us with a stable, reasoned response to the issues we encounter. Our emotions (including feelings, desires, wants, fears, etc.) are influences that guide our behaviors. However, the presence of emotion tends to push our thinking off-track and into all sorts of problematic ideas. As a result, in order to think clearly we need to find ways of keeping those confusing influences in check, while we work our way through the issue and see what's what. Just thinking, on the other hand, still happens when we are under confusing influences - which is why we can have very confused ideas even after thinking about them.

Imagine you are trying to add up a bunch of numbers in your head. Not that hard, but it requires some concentration. Now imagine someone in the room with you yelling out random numbers and blasting an airhorn in your ear. That's what emotion (various confusing influences) is doing while you're trying to think critically. The most effective first step is to figure out how to get away from that noise and interruption, and then, we can focus on making sure your arithmetic is solid.

These days (though I am sure every generation ever has thought the same thing), we are facing a severe moral confusion, which causes us to often be unable to think clearly. Moral confusion is a context where the emotional stress we face is amplified, because the issue we are facing can end up making us seem like moral monsters. It is a worse version of emotional confusion because the stakes seem even higher. When most every issue is presented as something to be outraged about - or to celebrate (while being outraged by something else), it becomes very difficult to get a solid grasp on the issue itself. If we agree, we are fascists; and if we disagree, we are Nazis. This makes for a very rough environment for critical thinking; and, at the same time, it is an environment where critical thinking is absolutely crucial.

---

1   Confusing here means something like, *ideas, feelings, thoughts and thought patterns that muddy the waters around the issue, making it difficult to make sense of.* We'll use the term **emotion** as a synonym.

Why should critical thinking be of such importance here?

As we will explore in later chapters, the proper use of reason gives us a stable foundation for everything we do. That foundation allows us to construct an orderly and functional understanding of ourselves, of the world, and the way that we (and our ideas) fit into the world. Moral confusion, on the other hand, creates a highly emotional context, where those emotional influences are very strong. That means that our ability to think clearly about these issues is severely reduced.

What exactly does that mean?

A stable foundation means something like a set of ideas that we can rely on; that we can fall back on when issues come up. The stability of reason means that reason itself does not change over time, or even person to person. $2+2 = 4$ is true now, and was true in the past; it is true for me and true for you. This gives us the reliability that what we have actually works (if used correctly), and it is the kind of thing that I can explain to you and you can explain to me.

Unstable foundations mean that ideas keep shifting, day to day, person to person. Instability means that you can't rely on these ideas, because they can disappear at any time. To give you an analogy, there is a reason we use concrete as a foundation for a house: concrete is stable. Building on sand is not a great idea precisely because the very ground on which you rely is constantly shifting. Similarly, when our ideas are orderly, that means that we understand the world in a way that lets us know what we need to do to get what we want - or what to do to avoid the outcomes we don't want.

For example, you may be reading this book as part of a college class you are taking. If you are an average student, you are reading this book, so that you may pass the class. You are taking the class to get college credit. You are getting that college credit so that you may graduate. You are probably trying to graduate so that you can be qualified for some kind of a job in the field you are interested in. You understand your goal, you understand how to get there. That's order.

Now imagine that you do everything you need for this class, and still fail; or you pass all your classes and get all the credits, but you are denied your degree; or you get your degree, but your entire field of interest no longer exists; etc.[2] These events throw us for a loop. Suddenly, we no longer understand what's going on (or maybe we never did). We no longer know how to go from where we are to where we want to be - how to act to get what we want. That is the opposite of order; that's chaos.

Clearly, stability and order are preferable to instability and chaos. This is also true when it comes to thinking. Sure, our **ideas** may change - especially as we get more information, learn new things, etc. - but the **process** of proper thinking does not change. That's where the stability and order come from. Let's use math for one more example here.

Let's say you see the problem: $100 - (3x4) = ?$ If you have not heard of the proper order of operations (PEMDAS), then you are likely to end up with $100-3 = 97x4 = 388$. Then, you learn about the order of operations and now you know that you should solve whatever is in the parentheses first. Your new answer is $100 - 12 = 88$.

The new answer is different, but the way that you do multiplication and subtraction did not change. All that happened is you learned a new piece of information, and it stacked on top of the information you already knew (the basic math functions). Although the original answer is wrong, the process for each step was correct. So, when you learn about PEMDAS, the stability and orderliness of your previous knowledge allows you to take in new information, and process it in ways that you already understood and could rely on.

When we learn how to create this stable and orderly foundation to our thinking, it becomes a new default setting for how we deal with ideas. It does not matter what the ideas are, the same way that it does not matter if you're adding up oranges or helicopters, because the underlying process (proper thinking) is the tool you are using to deal with the world. This also allows us to better deal with the emotionally confusing influences in our thinking. It does not matter what topic we are talking about, how sensitive it may be, etc. What matters is that we are thinking properly, clearly, and using reason in a way that allows us to communicate with other people in a way that we can all rationally understand.

---

2   I am sure that there was a person who got their Ph.D. is Soviet Studies, thinking they were set for a job for life - and a day later, the Soviet Union no longer existed, and all those jobs in Soviet Studies no longer existed. On a more recent note, there must have been some person who invested their life savings into opening up a business; then, a day later, the Covid shut-down closed their business - and they went bankrupt.

Whether we are adding up votes, victims, or people dancing for joy, 2+2 is still 4.

Moral, or generally emotional, confusion on any issue is a kind of interference with proper thinking. In our earlier analogy, it is the person yelling out random numbers and blowing the air horn while we're trying to focus on solving a problem. This undermines our ability to come to the correct conclusion, making those conclusions less stable and less orderly. Many of us have had the experience of performing a simple task under stress - like reading out loud in front of the class or public speaking. Suddenly, you start stuttering, mispronouncing words, or can't remember what you're supposed to do with your hands when you're talking. That's emotional confusion, and it clearly interferes with your ability to do the simplest tasks.

Arguably, the most important step to proper critical thinking is recognizing all those confusing influences for what they are, and learning how to deal with them in the most effective way. That is why the next two chapters are dedicated to drawing a clear line between reason and emotion.

SUMMARY

- Critical thinking is different from general "thinking," because it aims to get rid of emotionally confusing influences

- Emotional confusion is a context where the problems we face seem to introduce emotional stress in dealing with the issue.

- Moral confusion is a context where the emotional stress we face is amplified, because the issue we are facing can end up making us seem like moral monsters. It is a worse version of emotional confusion.

- Critical thinking creates a rational process that is stable and orderly, which strips off emotionally confusing influences, and which can easily be shared between people (the same way we can share the conclusion to 2+2).

    - Stable processes give us a foundation that is reliable because it does not change

    - Orderly processes let us understand how the world works, and how to act to get what we want (and how to act to avoid what we don't want).

- The alternative to critical thinking is unstable and chaotic situations, which keep shifting and changing, leaving us uncertain how to accomplish any of our goals.

CHAPTER 2

DECISIONS: EMOTION AND REASON

Every day we make thousands of decisions - up to 35,000 per day, by some calculations.[3] The difference in how we make decisions makes us different people; it creates different circumstances in which we work, it changes our context, and it opens and closes different doors to our future potential. So, how do we make these decisions? One useful way of approaching an answer to this question is to observe and understand the distinction between *reason* and *emotion*.

In the coming pages, we will try to draw the distinction between reason and emotion as clearly as we can. The goal is to ensure that we can recognize and properly deal with various emotional influences, to make our thinking as rational as possible. That said, the truth is that reason and emotion are closely in-

---

3   UNC-TV; Science. *How Many Daily Decisions Do We Make?* http://science.unctv.org/content/reportersblog/
choices#:~:text=It's%20estimated%20that%20the%20average,are%20both%20good%20and%20bad.

tertwined. Yes, we will present the distinction as a surgically clean line. However, the point is not that this distinction is somehow surgically precise in real life. Instead, we want to make a clear mental distinction between the two, because that is the most useful way to understand the differences in the kinds of thinking we do. You can think of it as a highly useful heuristic (mental shortcut), that will make the later material much easier to understand and implement.

This book focuses on the use of reason. In fact, for our purposes here, we want to completely remove emotion from the equation. That's not to say that emotions are bad or that a critical thinker needs to become a robot, rather, emotions should be under the control of reason, as will be explained shortly. So, let's take a look at what is meant by emotion and reason, and figure out why reason is the way to go.

Emotion

When we speak of emotions, we don't just mean something like feeling happy or sad. What we mean is the full spectrum of feelings, desires, wants, fears, etc. In this context, hunger is a kind of emotion. In fact, it is an emotional drive to find sustenance. It is built into you from birth. Fear is an emotion, so is pain. Emotions are socially and biologically implanted in us, and play a major part of our preferences and thinking.

That's great, but emotions also come with a whole set of their own problems. The most important of these problems, for us, is that **emotions are not in your control**. Emotions are not things you do; they are things that **happen to you**. And so, they come and go as they want, not as you want. Consider some examples:

- Look at this page. Now, feel attracted to it!
- Be happy! If that worked, psychologists would be out of a job. Never mind therapy, just "be happy" and not depressed!
- Just don't feel hungry and thirsty when you're dieting!

Emotions are essential to the way you relate to the world. Hunger is about wanting something from the world. Fear is about wanting to avoid something in the world. Depression is about the past not playing out as we wished. Anxiety is about being uncertain about the future, etc. Since you have no control over the world (as in, you can't just wish away reality - or wish reality into existing), you can't control whether or not you have an emotion or what that emotion is.

On top of that, emotions change all the time. You may have really been into *My Little Pony*, or *Dragonball-Z* as a kid; now you're not. You used to just love "Wheels on the Bus" but not anymore. Now you're into something else – you desire different things. Your favorite dessert changes, your favorite color, your favorite movie, tv show, etc. Your interests, your likes and dislikes, your preferences, who you are and are not attracted to – all of that changes in ways that you have no apparent control over. As a child, what did you want to be when you grew up? What major did you think you were going to have in college? At no point did you sit there and decide what you will like or dislike, what you will be afraid of, or not. You have no control at all over what emotions impinge upon you, and feelings often have a tendency of running amok.

This creates instability. You can't count on yourself to want or not want anything in the future. For example, when people get married, they're often crazy in love - yet, almost 50% of marriages end in divorce. What happened to that "crazy in love" status? People fall in love, and so they can just as equally fall out of it. There is no necessary rational justification for either of these events, they just happen.

Continuing on a pessimistic note, consider how often dating relationships fail. When we start dating, our emotions initially develop based on what we **imagine** the person is, not who they really are. That's because we don't know them enough to have feelings about who they really are. So, we project all sorts of ideas onto the other person, perhaps based on first impressions. After a while, we actually get to know them, and suddenly we discover that many of the ideas we had are unrelated to the person. Did you really love **that** person at the beginning? If they were never the kind of person we imagined them to be, who did we really love - a figment of our imagination? Plenty of people we saw as "wonderful" turned out to be terrible - think Ted Bundy or Bill Cosby.

By now, it should be evident that decisions that are made emotionally are incredibly unstable. They are unstable because those kinds of decisions depend on something that you have no control over, and that can change without warning. Unstable (emotional) decisions are far more likely to be short-lived and/ or negatively consequential (having a bad outcome), because the desire for doing or believing the thing (whatever the thing in question is) isn't constant, and you will no longer have a desire to believe or do that thing in the future.

Reason

In contrast to what we have described as emotion, reason is something you **can** control. You can use it to figure out what's true, what is best thing to do, how to act right, etc. And all you have to do is use reason. Of course, actually following through with reason is up to you. Emotion happens to you, but **you make reason happen**.

As an example, consider math. We understand math by reason, not by emotion. So when you see 2+2, you reason out the answer, you don't *feel* your way to it. Your emotions may be all over the place, but reason is reason. Reason does not change over time. 2+2= 4 was true when we first discovered it, it was true when you learned it, it is true today, and it will be true when the universe ends. You may learn new things that add to your rational understanding, like when you first learned that negative numbers are a thing and that you can, in fact, subtract 7 from 3. These new discoveries add to your knowledge, they don't somehow remove reason from the equation.

Reason is about **your understanding**. Because it is within your power, it can't change on you. You can try a little experiment. You rationally believe that 10>3. Now, ask yourself: *what would have to happen for me to stop believing this?* In the 12th century, Muhammad al-Ghazali (1058-1111 C.E.) - a famous theologian and philosopher - asked this question. As an exercise, he tried to come up with the most extreme example he could to make himself doubt what he knew:

> *...if I know that ten is more than three and then someone were to say: "No, on the contrary, three is more than ten, as is proved by my turning this stick into a snake" – and if he were to do just that and I were to see him do it, I would not doubt my knowledge because of his feat. The only effect it would have on me would be to make me wonder how he could do such a thing. But there would be no doubt at all about what I knew!*[4]

He is saying that if he meets someone who can change an *actual* stick into an *actual* snake – no illusion, real change of wood to snake and back – that would be very interesting, but it can't have any effect on reason and the knowledge that ten is actually more than three.

Reason does something that emotion cannot do: it gives us a stable point of reference from which

---

4   Al Ghazali, Muhammad. *Deliverance from Error*. Tr. R. J. McCarthy S.J.. Louisville; Fons Vitae, 1999. Pg. 20.

we can work. Reason is stable and does not change; it is unaffected by the kinds of things that happen to you. That is not to say that our ideas cannot change. Instead, the point is that the way we think – the **structure of that thinking** – does not change.

Continuing with the math example: we can have different solutions for different math problems. 2+2= 4, but 2+7= 9. However, the way we do math (the process of it) is the same - math and its rules do not change. The context of the problem changed, but the process did not. That's where the stability comes from, and this stability is the benefit of using reason over emotion in math (or whatever else we might apply reason to).

<u>Not a robot</u>

While we are pushing for reason over emotion, we need to be clear about something: emotions are not bad, we shouldn't get rid of them. Emotions are part of what makes you human. You need emotions as a guide to understanding the world. If you did not feel hunger, pain, fear, etc. you would not survive for very long. Emotions are, to a certain extent, what makes life worth living. However, because emotions are unstable, they are a bad basis for making responsible decisions.

Emotional decisions generally feel great in the moment, but they lead to problems down the line. Stress eating, drug use, screaming in an argument etc., all tend to be emotionally driven decisions. It is possible to make an emotional decision that ends up in agreement with reason, by pure chance. But, since the emotional decision is irrational, it has just as much chance to pick any other action and conclusion. This is part of what makes it so unreliable.

Unfortunately, we often tend to think that we're lucky enough that *feeling* our way to the correct answer is a viable option. However, if we look at this issue through a math analogy, we can see how big of a problem this kind of thinking really is. What is the answer to 2+2= ? There is exactly one correct answer to this question. You get to the right answer using reason and the rules of mathematics. That's how reason solves a problem. On the other hand, there is an *infinity* of numbers. That means that your odds of *guessing* the correct answer are one out of infinity. Which is to say, you have no chance of guessing your way to the correct answer. You need a guiding set of ideas to work it out, without which you are doing no better than guessing. The same holds for rational and emotional choices. The idea that you will *feel* your way to the rational answer has the same nonexistent odds.

So, how should we think of the relationship between emotion and reason? It is often useful, and interesting, to see how ideas work in different languages, because they let us see the idea with fresh eyes. Different languages develop ideas differently, and that gives us a new way of understanding old ideas. Also, if you're geeky enough, this is a fun activity.

So, let's look at how ancient Arabs understood it. The idea of reason and intellect in Arabic is the word *'AQL*. That word originally means the rope that the Arabs wear on their head – the rope that keeps down that red-white checkered scarf (*Kafiya*) men wear in Arabia.

The black rope is 'AQL

That rope had two main purposes: first, to keep the scarf from flying away in windy conditions; second, to tie down a camel when you are not riding. So, why did they pick that word for intellect and reason?

Imagine you ride your camel into town. You get off the camel and have some business to take care of. Can you just leave the camel waiting for you, like a parked car? No. Why not? Because it will wander off. Why would the camel go somewhere else, instead of waiting for you? Because it may be hungry, thirsty, it got scared, maybe she spotted a cute male camel… in short, because of desires. How do you prevent the camel from making your life miserable? You use the *'AQL* to tie the camel down. Now, the camel can't leave. It may experience all those desires we noted, but the desires are kept in check by that rope.

Desires are the kind of thing that interfere with your plans and can make your life miserable if you don't control them somehow. This is because you never know if/when they will strike and throw a wrench into your plans. So, the idea of "reason" in Arabic, is *a thing that is part of your head, that you use to keep the "animal desires" from running off and creating problems for you and everybody else.* Arabs, like many other people, use the terms "head" for reason and "heart" for emotions. Thus, the "part of your head" became linked to reason.

We can see the way that the emotions and desires of the camel were understood to be unstable forces. That meant that you could not count on them to be orderly and predictable. Instead, the Arabs had to find a way to place the emotions of the camel under control. Notice that they did not try to prevent the camel from having those emotions (that is impossible anyway), but instead they found a way to control how those emotions are expressed. By tying the camel, it is welcome to feel hungry, thirsty, afraid, etc. but it can't act out those emotions – because of the *'AQL.*

The same is true of the role of reason in regard to our emotions. You will have emotions, and you can't help that. Those emotions are ever-changing, unstable, and having those emotions is not something you can control. When you feel angry, you may want to assault someone. When you feel hungry, you just want to eat. When someone cuts you off on the highway, you want to run them off the road (or maybe that's just me). All of that is emotional, and that's fine. These are things you will feel, and you can't help it. However, what you can control is what you **do** about those emotions.

This is the role of reason. Reason is the way we can guide our behavior, which lets us control the ways in which we express our emotions. Some emotions we want to let through, and others we want to keep in check. When we are dieting, we keep our desire for food in check. When we need to go to the gym, but don't feel like getting off the couch, we can use reason to override that dislike of the gym. When we get to a restaurant hungry, we don't just take other people's food and start shoveling it into our mouths – even though that's what our emotions are telling us to do.

What about emotional choices in cases like love? Shouldn't we do things like get married out of love? Isn't that an emotional decision, the kind of a decision that we ought to be *feeling* our way through? Feeling love for a person is a nice thing, if you're planning to get married to them. But making the choice rationally is more important. What do we mean by "rationally" here? Making the choice rationally means that reason is actually in charge of making the choice. Your emotions make the suggestion, so to speak, but reason has the last word. If the other person is compatible with you, if they have the same kinds of long-term goals, the same kinds of values, if their vision of the future and yours are similar enough, if you share ideas about finances, about kids, etc. then marriage might be a rational choice.

Imagine if the other person's ideas about long-term goals are radically different from yours. Let's say, you want kids, and the other person loathes the very idea of children. While you may have passion for each other today, in a few years the realities of your differences will catch up to you. Those differences will mean suffering for both of you and, most likely, a divorce. Reason tells you this is a bad match for marriage, because the marriage is likely to break down (which is the opposite of why you are getting married).

You might be surprised just how many people don't go through these kinds of considerations. Whether it is kids, finances, or values and expectations, without a thoroughly rational take on these and other issues, emotional foundations are likely to crumble in the long run. So, while emotion is a good starting point for some decisions (like liking a person before considering marriage), it is not enough by itself. At least not for a stable set of decisions that can be used as a basis for grounding a life together and starting a family.

Our goal, ultimately, is to make sure that reason governs and guides emotion. You can't control what emotions you will have, but you can control how you act on that emotion. If emotions take over you, you will act passionately, but in irrational and often terrible ways. Murder is commonly the result of emotion; so is rape, assault, cheating, stealing, etc. We want to express our emotions in ways we find acceptable and that fit our ideas of who we should be and what the world should be like. To do that, we need to control our emotions by reason.

Emotional decision-making can insert itself in other areas of thought, even those where we believe that we are using reason. For instance, when the topic of abortion comes up, or some other hot button issue, most people simply stop thinking. Instead of reasonably considering the position being presented to them, the information they are hearing just becomes so much noise. In fact, they stop thinking to the point that they often can't even tell if a person is actually agreeing with them or not.

One of my favorite examples of this phenomenon comes from an article by Peter Singer on various arguments for and against abortion. The article is not taking a side, it is just listing all the arguments on both sides and explaining their benefits and drawbacks (yes, he has plenty for both sides). And yet, even though the article is not picking a side, about a third of readers will say that the author is "clearly a liberal pushing a liberal agenda;" and about a third will say that the author is "clearly a conservative pushing a conservative agenda."

Right there, you can tell that something went terribly wrong. How can people read the exact same article and come to such wildly different conclusions? The answer is that neither group was dealing with the article through reason. Instead, they were having a spasm of emotion based on the title (or maybe the first sentence or two of the article), and made a decision about it without consulting their ability to reason.

We all do this, to some extent or another, far more often than we would like to admit. If we hear something negative about ourselves or someone/something we like, we get defensive. When we hear something positive, we agree. How often do fans of a sports team scream at the ref when the call is against their team? Even when replay clearly shows that the ref made the right call? This is another example of emotionally "feeling" your way through a situation, and failing miserably.

Reaction and Response

So far, we examined the relation between emotions and reason. We now turn to a practical side of how those two features work when we deal with ideas. When dealing with people, ideas, things, etc. the most common style of engagement we use is reaction. That is, when we are confronted by something – a claim, a statement, an idea, position, ideology, etc. – we seek to engage it immediately; usually by either defending our own against the new ones, or by trying to attack the confronting concept. Alternatively, if the issue is in line with our own feelings, we react by agreeing with it. A reactionary position is indicative of being surprised, unprepared, and generally working on the fly. Generally speaking, action is preferable to reaction.

Within the context of an argument, heated or not, the problem with reacting is that the other party decides on timing and rules of engagement. They get to bring up their position at whatever point and in whatever way they feel is most advantageous to them, and they force us to deal with their claims as they come. Deepening the disadvantage, reaction is often accompanied by the influence of emotional imbalance - as is the case when someone opens up by "pushing your buttons." When we are emotionally disturbed by claims, arguments, or attacks, then we go on the defensive, our cognitive functions become impaired (the rational part of ourselves starts shutting down), and we perform poorly. This is why people can say things in the heat of the moment that they would never consider saying otherwise.

An alternative to reaction is response. For our purposes:

A response is a calm, measured, and well-informed approach to encountering an issue, claim, or argument. It implies a kind of cessation of one side, before the other side engages.

This difference can be seen easily in the political realm. Consider the difference between pundits yelling over one another - when it is clear that neither side can even hear the other, let alone understand them - as opposed to a written response to an issued statement. The benefit of responding, instead of reacting, is that it gives us the time to take in all the information, fully process it, and – most importantly – examine the kinds of assumptions, implications, and ideas that are inherent to the initial claims.

If you just jump into answering a question, you end up accidentally accepting all sorts of ideas you do not find acceptable. For example, the reactionary answer to the question, "Do you still beat your spouse?" is a "No!" That's the trick with reacting – you end up accepting the built-in assumptions. In this case, the built-in assumption is that you were previously abusive. Or imagine that your significant other walks up to you and asks, "are you going to apologize?" Both "yes" and "no" answers are a bad option. The question itself assumes your guilt. Answering "yes" confirms it, answering "no" assumes your innocence. Both are emotional reactions. But, if you are not absolutely certain what the issue is, you don't know whether you are guilty or innocent. Instead, asking the other person to clarify what they think you have done wrong, is the way to go - since that gives you the clarity to know whether you are, in fact, guilty or not. Because responding is about sitting back and examining these ideas first, it is a much better way of making sure you don't accidentally say a bunch of things you don't mean to say. A response to the first question would be something like, "I never have beat my spouse," or "What makes you think I ever beat my spouse?" These responses at least challenge the underlying assumptions that the reactionary answer simply accepts.

Al Ghazali (the same one mentioned earlier) brought out this difference in his *Deliverance from Error*, where he criticized people for reacting and engaging in argument and debate without understanding exactly what's going on. Their reactionary approach could not solve the issues they faced; it only created additional chaos and confusion, because they had no understanding of the issues. Instead, Al Ghazali argues that in order to fully respond to an idea, we must first become as knowledgeable about that idea as its **best proponents**. As an example, Al Ghazali held that a theologian who wants to engage in criticizing a philosophy, needs to first get his Ph.D. in philosophy (and vice versa). Otherwise, their ignorance of the issue merely causes confusion.

Imagine a bunch of random people trying to tell a surgeon that they *feel* that the way surgery is done is wrong, and that the surgeon should instead do this *other* thing they came up with, instead. We do not think this is a kind of idea that should be taken seriously, because the random people are not experts. That is, we don't think that non-experts should be meddling into areas where expertise is needed. For our purposes, you need not pause to go back to school; however, you must do everything you can to fully understand the claim before trying to engage.

The reason for this approach, Al Ghazali argues, is that this in-depth learning does two things: First, it allows us to understand the arguments from the inside – in the way that the best supporters of that position would understand them. This prevents our response from being superficial, or from failing to fully connect by lacking the total awareness of the argument structure. Second, the in-depth study also allows us to find the internal cracks of the position. This gives us serious leverage in constructing our response. Whether we want to break the idea or try to fix it, we first have to know what exactly we are dealing with.

You can think of it this way: When you are confronted with a household problem – say, an A/C unit that's not working as it should – you don't simply grab a hammer and start hitting various surfaces around your house, in hopes that the problem will be resolved. You don't even concentrate on hitting the A/C unit. Instead, you check the thermostat, whether the power is on, maybe check the breaker to make sure that it's not just the A/C unit that's off. Then, depending on how DIY you happen to be, you call an expert or start looking at Google, Reddit, and YouTube for ways to diagnose and fix the issue. This kind of response engages the problem as it is, not as we might hope it to be, and focuses our attention to the areas and methods most likely to generate the desired outcome, i.e. a cool house.

In abstract, this process is just you working your way down a list of things which you actually know, to check if you understand the problem. When you no longer know what to do, and the problem is not resolved, you either call someone with expertise for the given problem or go off to become more knowledgeable yourself. That makes sense in every practical problem you have ever faced. What makes no sense is randomly acting out, with no regard for knowledge on the issue. Reactions are, essentially, temper tantrums in hopes that something about your screaming and thrashing fixes the problem.

Consider the following: in the abortion debate, people define their own side as "pro-life," or as "pro-choice." But if we think about it for a second, those terms are actually intended to say something about anyone who might disagree with the position that's being presented (which makes them "loaded terms"). If Bob is pro-life, and you think his argument is bad (maybe Bob is really bad at presenting his ideas), then you are "against life." That makes you "pro-death!" At least, that's what the term here is intended to imply. We see this with the terms that get thrown around, like "murderer," or "baby-killer." The same is true of the other side. If Steve is pro-choice, then disagreeing with Steve is going to be labeled as "anti-choice." If we look at the less polite version of that phrase, we see terms like "tyranny, dictator, pro-slavery," and references to the *Handmaid's Tale*.

The truth is never that simple. I have met plenty of people who have issues with certain parts of both pro-life and pro-choice positions or arguments. And yet, they were most certainly not "pro-death" or "pro-slavery." When issues come up - especially hot button topics - we tend to just jump in without examining the underlying assumptions we have been given by the other side. Without examining those underlying assumptions, we get easily tricked into defending ideas we have no interest in defending. However, because the other side decided on the rules of the engagement, and we bought into them by reacting, we got stuck with someone else's ideas. We can avoid all of that by shifting to a rational, response-based approach, instead of the emotional, reaction-based one. Yes, even when the other side is literal Nazis (and they almost never are).

Reactions are easy, because they are emotionally charged. We react when someone "pushes our buttons" – and we lose our cool and just start lashing out. Responses are hard, specifically because the first step of a response is reigning in our emotional, ego-driven reactions, and only then turning to the issue with reason. Obviously, depending on the issue, our emotions may or may not flare up, and the degree of emotional response differs. However, keeping our cool is a matter of practice, and we are all capable of it when the situation demands it. Getting into the habit of responding, instead of reacting, gives us the best chance of addressing the problems we face.

This distinction is important, not only in terms of your own behavior, but also the behavior of others. When a big story breaks, there is a media rush to draw viewers to it and get eyeballs on screens. Since story X is trending, a lot of additional content will be generated to piggyback off the first story. As a result, later articles by other authors will assume the truth of the initial story X, and then "spin yarn" on any additional angle that can be derived. This propagation of stories comes with its own set of sources, experts, and vague ideas floating about the digital ether. These will, in turn give rise to a set of tertiary stories, and so forth. These unreflective, reactionary stories might generate the views and clicks desired by the media outlets that publish them, but fail to offer insight into the initial story or add to it in any useful way.

What is happening here is a chain-reaction. The ideas of the initial story are accepted in a reaction, and everyone else proceeds on the basis of that being true. A better way to engage with the story would be to craft a response: a carefully considered and researched approach to understanding the first story. This would result in a clear and lucid understanding of the initial story, and provide readers with a more focused and useful secondary story; exactly what the reactionary stories seem uninterested in doing (most secondary articles are little different than banging a hammer on every surface of the house to fix the A/C, because they're primarily there for the clicks).

On the individual level, in the chaos of such a media storm, being able to identify and categorize reaction stories as just that, mere reactions, puts you in a place of privilege to seek or craft a genuine response to the initial story. In such circumstances it might be that, not only do you have a better personal understanding of the events as they are actually happening, but **everyone else got it wrong, and you got it right.** That insight also gives you an advantage in all sorts of other areas.

In these cases, it is all the more important to refuse to react. Only the calm and rational response is likely to produce desirable results. If the problem is real, and the A/C is out (or, the media is in a blitz), then how you decide to engage with it must be fully considered before you decide to interact. If you react instead of respond, based on emotion and "instinct," you lose the chance to reason your way through the issue and must restart your approach after your reaction has proved itself unsuitable. Worse yet, your reaction is likely to lead you to believe that you actually know what is going on, when you don't have a clue. This makes it far less likely that you will go back and reconsider your original position. On top of that, your reaction will add to the bandwagon effect, and you will influence others to have an emotional reaction, instead of thinking clearly (whether they agree or disagree with you). That is, you will make the problem worse for yourself and others. We must always be aware that the problem of reaction and response is not only a problem for us but also a problem for everyone around us.

Conclusion

In this chapter we have made a distinction between two major methods of engaging with information in the world and making decisions from it. The two major tools we have at our disposal for decision-making are **Emotion** and **Reason**. These two are distinguished by both the way they appear in our minds and the results they produce. Emotions are things that happen to you. They are uncontrollable in their appearance or disappearance. This results in unstable decisions and beliefs, which can shift unpredictably, with no warning, based on uncontrollable inputs. Alternatively, reason is something that you do, and that you can control. Reason follows rules and guides you to stable conclusions that can grow with new information, but will not change without rationally integrated new information. Emotions are always part of the equation. While we can't control what emotions we have, we can control what we do about them. That control is done by reason. In the next chapter, we will explore how rational and emotional options play out in decision-making.

SUMMARY

We have two tools for making decisions, which give us two ways we can deal with incoming ideas: **Emotion/Reaction** or **Reason/Response.**

- **Emotion** is:
    - What happens to you
    - Uncontrollable (you don't get to decide to have it or not)
    - Unstable (it can change on its own, at any moment)
    - Uses **Reactions**

- **Reactions** are:
    - Fast (instinctual, animalistic lashing out)
    - Emotional (because they are not rational)
    - Unstable
    - Buy into the assumptions of the idea that is presented to us
    - Reactions are dangerous, because we don't have the time to fully understand the idea before engaging it – we trade accuracy for speed.

- **Reason** is:
    - What you do
    - Controllable (you decide to act on it, or not)
    - Stable (does not change, or change comes rationally with new information)
    - Uses **Responses**

- **Responses** are
    - Slower (rational, evaluative, processing)
    - Rational (careful consideration of all things)
    - Stable
    - Evaluate every part of the idea that is presented to us
    - Responses are slower and less aggressive, because we sit back and carefully sift through every part of the idea, making sure we fully understand everything, before we engage – we trade speed for surgical precision.

- While we can't control what emotions we have, we can control what we do about them. That control is a function of reason.

CHAPTER 3

MORAL AND FUNCTIONAL SCALES

In the preceding chapter, we focused on separating emotion and reason, and the way we use that distinction to understand reactions and responses. In this chapter, we want to focus on how moral confusion enters our thinking, and how to address that sort of interference. Moral confusion is the emotional interference that comes from a feeling of moral disturbance - when the idea we are faced with seems to be strongly related to our beliefs about right and wrong.

For example, most of us don't have a problem if someone asks us, hypothetically, "what's wrong with being sick?" If we think about it, we can conclude that this question is actually asking us why sickness is defined as bad and health as good, and perhaps that can lead into a conversation about the rights and responsibilities of sick people and the society. However, if we turn the same hypothetical question into, "what's wrong with rape?" we suddenly have a much stronger and clearly emotional reaction from almost every person. Notice here that the question did not argue that rape is good, any more than the first question argued that sickness is good. But the idea of rape is so morally repugnant, that as soon as it comes up, we seem to stop thinking and start reacting.

In our case, we want to look at a more abstract version of this problem so that we can better understand what it is about moral language that triggers the emotional reactions, and how to avoid it. Specifically, we are interested in comparative value claims – statements that deal with something being "better" or "worse" – especially when considering people or some features of attitudes, behaviors, and ideas that are related to varying cultures.

We will do this by establishing the two ways that we make comparative value statements: statements made on the **moral scale** and statements made on the **functional scale**.

Before we begin, I want you to think about how you (and the society around you) are likely to perceive statements like, "Steve is better than Shanice," or "Women are better than men," or "Germans are better than South Africans." Each of those statements is a comparative value claim - it states that X is better/worse etc. than Y. What do you think about statements like this? Are they good, bad, or neutral? Why do you think that?

Since roughly the civil rights era in the U.S. (1954-68), there has been a lot of talk about equality – specifically the need to meaningfully affirm the equality of people regardless of their race, gender, ethnicity, creed, ability, etc. Obviously, that conversation was started much earlier, but it was the 1960s that saw the issue reach a critical point in the consciousness of the general population. This culminated in the Fair Housing Act (1965), Equal Employment Opportunity Act (1972), and other such measures designed to legally affirm and protect the equality of the various groups, and individuals within those groups within the United States.

However, since roughly the 1990's, the push for equality has taken on a rather different direction. In particular, a primary concern of the equality conversation seems to have become centered on the notion that pointing out differences in individuals or groups should be considered an attempt to undermine the equality of people (with the exception of identifying differences in order to celebrate them). This move to eliminate the recognition of differences between groups and individuals is a bad one, rationally speaking, for a number of reasons. However, we begin with a few caveats.

First, it is relevant to note that the emphasis of *differences* among people – drawn along any number of identity lines (such as race, gender, etc.) – has historically been used to justify actual oppression, up to and including genocide, of those considered "different" in a way that made them somehow "inferior." Consider, for example, the European slave trade, the Nazi Final Solution, the Rwandan genocide of the Tutsi by the Hutu, or the Bosnian genocide of the Bosnian Muslims by the Eastern Orthodox Serbs (that one used two points of difference - ethnicity and religion). As soon as people are primarily identified by some identity group, rather than as individuals, there exists a potential that the trait used to define that group can be used to condemn all its members. By condemning the group trait (including race, ethnicity, or whatever), it is possible to pass judgment on all individuals in that group, without trial, evidence, or accounting for the realities of individual actions and responsibility. That is, we have a basis for collective guilt, and justification for collective punishment. As incoherent as that may sound, this attitude has especially been the case in the West, which had used the idea of differences in peoples to justify natural slavery.[5] Therefore, it is somewhat understandable that the idea of accepting differences, or maybe even emphasizing them, is a sensitive one.

Second, in this chapter we are not attempting to undermine, in any way, the notion of equality of humans as humans. Instead, the aim is to preserve this equality while allowing for a pragmatic ability to acknowledge the kinds of functional differences that are undeniably present, and which must be accounted for, if society is to continue to function. This, as will be seen, is an important feature of properly responding (instead of reacting) to and evaluating ideas.

While keeping these caveats in mind, let's consider the notion of a moral scale. As a side note, the actual points on the graphs below are arbitrary (except for the occasional specific point being made - e.g. cows in *Figure 2*). The specific ordering is generally culturally designated, and is not intended as a sort of hard and fast, inflexible, hierarchy. The fact that there is ordering happening is what is important (as an exercise for the reader, consider how those orders might change if this book were published in different parts of the world).

---

5   Aristotle. *Politics*. http://www.wright.edu/~christopher.oldstone-moore/Aristotleslavery.htm

Moral Scales

Let us begin by defining the first term:

Moral value is the intrinsic value of an entity; the value that is independent of the use derived by others from that entity, and which determines its rights and responsibilities.

Moral value is granted to beings in different gradations (different levels) and comes with differing rights and responsibilities. In nearly all human thought, and especially in the Western experience, humans are the only entities with true moral value, and have a lion's share of rights and responsibilities. We can imagine the moral scale (*Figure 1*) as a way of organizing the world. The higher up on the moral scale we go, the more rights a thing has. Thus, it is not a problem to treat insects as "pests" and attempt to eradicate them, but it is a problem to treat our pets in the same way. This is why you can kill a mosquito at your neighbor's barbecue without consequence, but you can't just squish their labradoodle Fluffy and act like nothing happened.

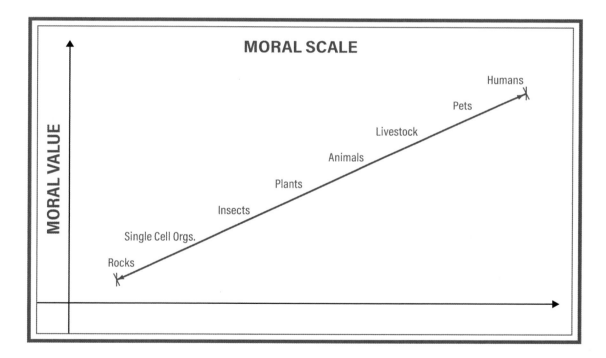

Figure 1

The primary distinction of the moral scale occurs between human (top) and non-human (everything else). The ability of humans to tell right from wrong is taken as the reason why humanity is set apart. From the Judeo-Christian perspective, which became the standard Western position, whatever is under humans on the moral scale is subject to some form of use (or exploitation) by humans.[6] This follows historically from the reading of Genesis 2, with the idea that the value of non-humans is determined by their utility to humanity.[7] As a result, we can think of the simplified moral scale as humans (with all the rights and responsibilities) at the top, and sub-humans, with limited rights and no/few responsibilities, underneath. So long as others are at our own level on the moral scale, they have the same rights and responsibilities as we do, by definition. Thus, their treatment must be the same kind of treatment we would consider acceptable for ourselves. All other entities are sub-human, and subject to our use, exploitation, desires, care, stewardship, etc.

A good example of applying this simplified moral scale can be seen in the idea of food. Generally, humans are morally able to consume all non-humans as food. There are occasional dietary prohibitions, depending on specific people or groups, but, generally speaking, all non-humans are on the menu. This also includes pets, in cases of emergency, though they are far above the rest of the entries on the moral scale. However, the one thing that is never on the menu, are other humans. Even in extreme situations, killing a human being for food is an inexcusable sin in Western society. Even consuming a human that died of natural causes is greatly frowned-upon. If you do it, and we catch you, you are going to have a very bad go of it.

By comparison, the animal world is not limited in their diets – because they have no responsibility other than biological drives for survival. Thus, when an animal eats a human, it is not a morally bad animal – because it has no responsibilities not to eat certain foods to begin with. This lack of responsibility even goes as far as including eating the young of their own species – as is the case with praying mantises, hamsters, lions, etc. Again, we do not pass judgments on animals for such actions, though we are likely to summarily execute any human that did such a thing.[8]

6   White, Lynn. "The Historical Roots of Our Ecological Crisis [with discussion of St. Francis; reprint, 1967]." Ecology and Religion in History. New York: Harper and Row, 1974.

7   *Ibid.* Excluding God and angels.

8   While cannibalism is a known historical activity of some tribes, no major civilization has ever allowed it (i.e. large,

In certain instances, we do appear to pass judgment on animals who consume humans, because we hunt them down and kill them. However, this is not a *moral* judgment against the animal, but a *practical* one. A tiger who turns man-eater is not hunted because it is morally deficient, but because it threatens the survival of other humans in the area. The tiger is neither "allowed" to eat people, nor is it "prohibited" from eating people, because it's a tiger and not high enough on the moral scale to have such responsibilities. In contrast, people are allowed to kill the tiger, precisely because humans are understood to outrank the tiger on the moral scale. Therefore, the survival of humans takes precedence over the survival of the tiger.

Another great example of applying the moral scale is the diet at work in Hinduism. As a matter of religious perspective, cows are understood to be sacred in Hinduism. That is, their moral value (rights of cows) has been elevated from the standard understanding in the rest of the world, which considers them as simple livestock. Once this upgrade kicks in (*Figure 2*), the cow is suddenly off the menu. In fact, eating beef is, in Hinduism, equivalent to cannibalism – if not worse.

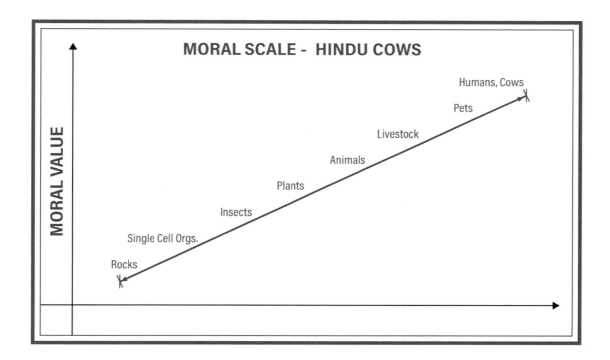

Figure 2

long-lasting civilization).

Not all alterations to the moral scale have been so innocuous. Historically, the notion of slavery in the West has rested, to some degree, on the belief that the enslaved populations belong to the sub-human category (*Figure 3*). Perhaps, it is more accurate to say that, following Aristotle's position on natural slavery,[9] the slave is seen as an inferior human, and the master is seen as a superior human. In either case, it is this reduction in humanity that has made the slave susceptible to mistreatment unto death.[10]

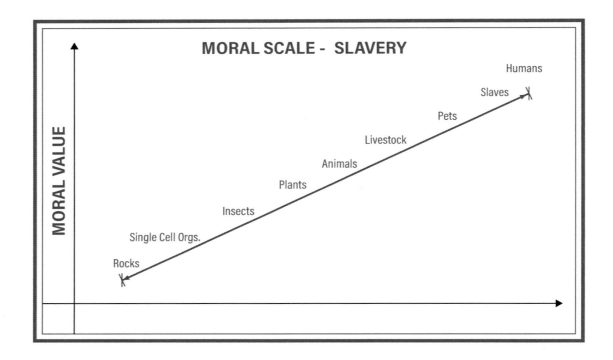

Figure 3

A similar line of reasoning was generally used in justifying colonial treatment of local populations.[11] Crucially, the idea that permeated the colonial mindset is that the people who were colonized were inferior humans. Thus the superior humans had the right to treat the colonized people as they saw fit, by the virtue of their ability to militarily defeat the locals. That is, those who could militarily win were understood to be superior to the people who ended up defeated. *Figure 4* shows a potential ordering for the relevant areas of the moral scales acted upon by colonizers in much of Western history.

---

9   Aristotle. *Politics*. 1254b 16-21.

10   Plato. "Euthyphro." In *The Works of* Plato. Ed. Irwin Edman. New York; The Modern Library, 1956. Pp. 37-9.

11   Mill, J.S. *A Word on Non-Intervention*. London: Foreign Policy Perspectives #8. 1859. Pg. 4.

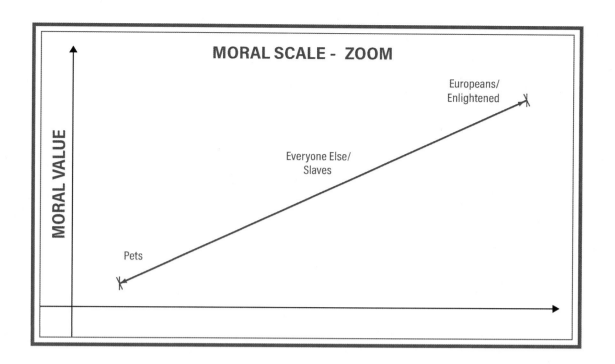

Figure 4

The colonial moral scale ideology was taken to its extreme point by the Nazis, who, like jingoistic and xenophobic tribes, admitted only themselves to the highest level of the moral scale. The real trick in the Nazi position of Aryan supremacy was not the claim that *some* humans are more human than others. Indeed, this had been an accepted notion in Europe, the U.S., and elsewhere, for quite a while. In fact, a number of European peoples under the reign of other Europeans fared little better than American slaves had (for example, see the Irish under British rule). The real trick with the Nazis was the elevation of all German people above all other people, including all other Europeans, in the same way that the Europeans in general saw themselves above the people they had colonized.

This was a rather serious change from the earlier animosity. In general, there was a recognition of human value between adversaries. Consider the British and the French who were at war for centuries. The British crown would have gladly wiped out the French nobility and vice versa, but they saw the common people as people – and in case of victory, those people would be under conditions functionally no different than their own people of equal rank (a French peasant was no different than a British peasant, because they just did peasant things). The idea of Aryan supremacy made all non-Aryans inferior, and thus sub-human on the moral scale (*Figure 5*). This means that even other Europeans were subject to the issue of moral inferiority. Of course, this is an oversimplified account, but it gets the general point across.

This act of reducing the intrinsic value of other humans is commonly called "othering," and is the first step towards the ability to commit genocide against the people that are now somehow less human.[12] This is because we are unhappy to be exterminating other **humans**, but if we can start seeing them as less than human, then it becomes acceptable to do terrible things to them.

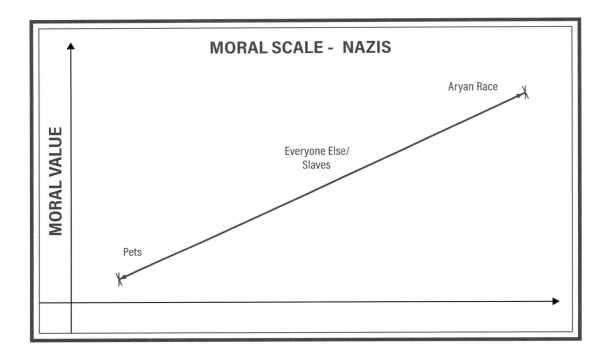

Figure 5

The moral scale separates all things into the human and non-human groups and assigns them moral value. Recall, moral value is the intrinsic value of an entity, which determines its rights and responsibilities, and that moral value is granted to things at different levels and comes with differing rights and responsibilities. The modern "equality" position started as an attempt to ensure that all humans are part of that top-tier spot with equal rights. This way, we would not engage in "othering" people due to charac-

---

12   Stanton, Gregory H. *10 Stages of Genocide*. http://genocidewatch.net/genocide-2/8-stages-of-genocide/

teristics like race, ethnicity, gender, etc. However, over time, many claims and references to differences, including the glaringly obvious biological ones, began to be perceived as somehow attempting to remove the **moral equality** of those who are "different."

If we treat all references to differences of individuals or groups as claims about the moral scales of those individuals or groups, we are likely to react where we should not. This is because every notion of difference between people is something we will see as step one towards descending into Nazism. However, the moral scale is not the only one in play. That means that there is another way to think of claims about differences. We need to be able to tell the difference between the kinds of statements being made, and what scale they are using, or we will simply keep on reacting, instead of responding.

Functional Scale

The functional value measures practical value - the problem-solving ability of a thing; how useful something happens to be for accomplishing some specific task, in a specific way.

Practical or functional value (terms are interchangeable) is an attribute that is entirely unrelated to moral value. In fact, depending on the situation in which we measure practical value, the position on the scale will change for the same object.

A basic, and very abstract, view of practical value might look something like the hierarchy depicted in *Figure 6*. As a more concrete example, we can think of the idea that we have developed different tools, specifically because they are different in how well they can solve different problems. A screwdriver can solve screwdriver problems; but a multi-tool can solve screwdriver problems and a bunch of other ones as well. So, the multi-tool might have a higher practical value.

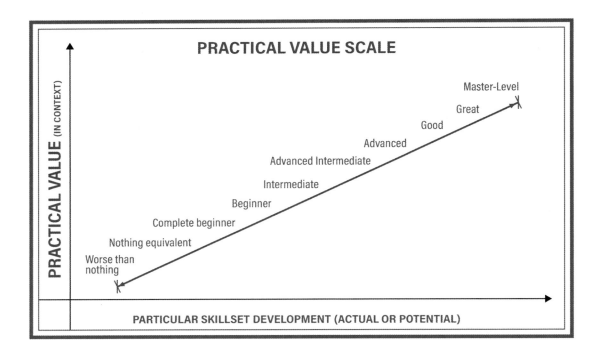

Figure 6

Clearly, the **context of need** can flip the entire practical ranking on its head, because the kinds of problems we need to solve change radically. For example, landing a man on the moon (as a problem in need of a solution) required a whole lot of people whose skill sets included mathematics, engineering, etc. Thus, the people with those skills had greater practical value in that context. On the other hand, that same group of top-notch scientists is probably not a practical group to rely on when we want information about the latest fashion trends, or if we need a top-notch farmer. If we need someone to run across a battlefield, dodging bullets the whole way to deliver orders to friendly troops under fire, Stephen Hawking, for all his brilliance, is simply at the bottom of the list of practical value (both because he was wheelchair bound, and because he is no longer alive).

Practical value is a field where the **differences** between individuals or groups become exactly the kind of thing we want and need to know, if we want to achieve success in whatever endeavor we are engaged in at the time. It allows us to best identify the kinds of potential most likely to contribute to the best problem-solving outcome. The Navajo, for example, had a particularly high practical value in WWII precisely because of a feature of being Navajo – namely their language which was resistant to code-breaking attempts by the Axis powers. This gave them far higher value in the war than their relatively limited numbers would otherwise suggest.

Oddly enough, the question of practical value is so radically different from that of moral value, that it easily crosses the species boundary. Keep in mind that, on the moral scale, there was no way for a different species to be temporarily considered higher than a human being. But when we are looking at the practical scale, the functional value of an ox greatly exceeds that of a human, in the context of tilling fields in a pre-mechanized era. That does not mean that I can't eat the ox. Dogs have far greater value than most humans, in the contexts of finding avalanche survivors, etc. The context of our problem has a significant impact on the practical value scale we apply. Bob may be a terrible driver, but a great dancer – so he is at the bottom of the hierarchy of skilled drivers, but at the top of the hierarchy of skilled dancers. The way we *practically* understand these people and their skills depends on the context of our needs. If I need a dancer, Bob is a great choice. If I need a driver, he is the worst choice. Notice that Bob's humanity is never in question (I can't eat Bob because he's a bad driver); only his skills are in question, and those depend on the specific context of what is needed.

Examples like this make it clear that conflating the moral and practical scales is incoherent. The fact that Bob is a worse dancer than Steve is a difference between the two, and focusing on that difference is the morally right thing to do if we need the best dancers we can get. This does not make Steve more human, nor does it make Bob sub-human. Any attempt to read the statement this way is missing the point.

Additionally, these examples highlight the importance of acknowledging differences: a company looking to sort through 100 applications needs to pay attention to the *differences* between the applicants, keeping in mind the needs of their companies for specific problem-solving practical value. The equality of those applicants, in terms of their humanity and human rights, is irrelevant for this task. When I want someone to look over my philosophy article, I contact a different friend than when I'm looking to fix my car. I know who to contact for which job by focusing on the **differences of practical value** between individuals in this specific context. This does not mean that I imagine one friend as sub-human, in order to get help from another, just that I know that one friend is practically better at offering help with my issue than the other.

The question of practical value is a question rooted in the specifics of our goals, or the hierarchy of goals we happen to have - thus, the aforementioned context of need. The qualities that matter in assigning practical value are entirely dependent on the goal in question. Without defining the goal, we cannot functionally distinguish between the practical value of Stacey and a rock. To borrow an analogy from Al Ghazali, there is no such thing as "sickness" and no such thing as "medicine." All sicknesses are actually specific conditions, and all medicines are actually specific treatments. Knowing what treatment is required is a matter of knowing what condition is to be treated. We cannot coherently argue that all medicines are equal, because they treat "sicknesses," and thus that it should make no difference what pills we take.

This flexibility of application in practical value scales leads to one of it's very interesting and important features: **it is not actually set in stone** by the virtue of some given attribute of a person. It can, and does change, based on the kinds of activities that are up to the individual – like dedication to work, conscientiousness, corruptibility, etc. For example, something like high IQ is a potentially valuable feature. But not all high IQ people perform to their potential. In fact, if high IQ is not paired with something like a strong work ethic, the results are significantly sub-par.

A high IQ student who does not put in the time throughout the semester and writes the final paper hours before it is due, produces a worse product than a classmate with lower IQ but great work ethic. This is the *Tortoise and the Hare* scenario, and the value produced by the proverbial tortoise is actually far higher (so long as the race is something the tortoise is physically capable of accomplishing). The practical value scale can, and does, take such effort-based aspects into account when producing the final analysis of practical value (for a given set of circumstances for a given individual). Obviously, effort is not always enough to make a difference. Someone missing a crucial feature cannot simply make up for it by hard work, and so no amount of effort helps. For example, if the minimum height requirement for a rollercoaster tester is 6'4", there is no amount of effort that will get me there if I'm 5'9".

The practical value scale also has to take into account the drives and intentions of the groups or individuals in question, which is not something we do in the moral value scale. Simply being an expert in a field, or having a high IQ is not enough to be practically valuable in all situations. Dr. Josef Mengele was a great medical doctor (in terms of skill), who was also a dedicated Nazi and a kind of monster normally reserved for only the most terrifying mythologies. While he would certainly be capable of treating your sore throat, his drives and intentions make him less than suitable for family practice, and far more suited for the gallows. Therefore, practical value scale must also account for the group or individual functionality within society (through concepts like socialization).

Humans function primarily in societies, and societies require us to rely on the practical function-ality of others to satisfy certain needs we have, but are unwilling or unable to attend to ourselves. This is why most of us don't grow our own food, despite the fact that food is necessary for each individual's survival. Instead, we have outsourced the problem to someone else, and trade for goods in labor (generally represented as money – the outcome of that labor). Consequently, we see each other as human, yes, but also as the kinds of things we use to accomplish our own goals. Again, **practical value is independent of moral value**. A human is a human, with the full range of rights assigned to them. Their practical value is a function of their active and potential contribution to the problem-solving capacity in this context, not their humanity. We should not confuse the two scales, and there is no objective problem with having a frank and open discussion on the question of individual and group differences. In fact, the exploration of these differences plays a major part in our daily interactions with others.

If we're going to be able to make rational decisions, we need to insist on the fact that there are differences, and that identifying and focusing on them is not an attack on the moral status of different people. Otherwise, the result is that we have to pretend that Yao Ming and Steve the pygmy are identical in all ways. No, they're not. One is 7'6" and the other is 4'11". If height is what happens to play a role in functional problem-solving at the moment (maybe we need to reach the top shelf, or maybe we need someone to fit into an A/C duct), pretending that there is no difference between the two is incoherent, and actively hurts our ability to solve the problems before us. Imagine trying to claim that, since a hammer and a screwdriver are both tools, there is no difference in which one you use. Perhaps if the problem can be solved by either screwing in the screw, or hammering it in, that would be fine. But if the problem facing us is the disassembly of your brand-new laptop, suddenly the differences between a hammer and a screwdriver are critical to note.

CONCLUSION

The distinction between moral and practical scales, which then gives us moral and practical statements, is an important one. It is understandable to have an emotional reaction when some difference in people (groups or individuals) is pointed out. This might be because we assume that the difference is supposed to be a moral one – which would mean that we're calling someone sub-human. But, since we actually have two very different scales, we must be careful not to confuse what's happening. Whether a statement sounds offensive or not, the key is to respond, not react. Practical value statements must be understood as functional – without a moral component.

Understanding the difference between moral and functional values is an important step to correctly identify and prevent emotional reactions from taking off. Moral confusion is a very common way that we end up with a lot of emotional interference with our reason. The confusion commonly comes up because we understand an idea in a moral, instead of a practical, way. Now that we know that there is a difference, and that we can speak about practical differences without making moral judgments, we will be able to make that distinction in any ideas we encounter, in order to better respond to them - and to do so in the most effective way.

An easy way to get sidetracked when looking at a claim or idea is to get the moral and practical claims confused. We tend to have very strong emotional reactions about moral differences between people – and rightly so. However, the fact that differences are brought up, or are a key feature of an idea, does not necessarily make it a moral claim. While it is *possible* to misuse differences as the basis for claiming greater or lower moral value of individuals or groups (as it is possible to misuse all things), that does not mean that pretending that there are no differences is a rational thing to do. Making sure that we are focused on the practical scales, and not moral ones, is a good way to limit our own reactions.

We must be careful to distinguish between these two scales. When we encounter an idea, no matter how repugnant, we have to take that step back and stop reacting. We must respond, and discover whether the idea is actually about moral value or practical value. The same is true of the way that we express ourselves; we must be careful not to confuse practical values with moral values in our ideas, and to ensure that we communicate clearly to our audience which scale we are using.

With that, we have come to the end of our first section. We have examined emotion and reason, the ways in which the two create different behaviors (reactions and responses), and have considered some important ways in which to prevent emotions from clouding our judgment. In the next section, we will consider how ideas do and don't work, how arguments are structured, and begin to see how they can be taken apart for better analysis.

SUMMARY

- Moral claims are about the intrinsic values of human beings – their rights and responsibilities.

- Whatever is below you on the moral scale is the kind of thing that has less rights and responsibilities than you do, and it could be sacrificed - if need arose.

- Functional claims are about the functional value of everything in the world – how useful it is for solving the specific problem we are dealing with right now.

- Whatever is below you on the practical scale, is simply worse than you at doing this specific job. Whatever is above you, is better at it.

- If we mistake a functional idea for a moral one, we are more likely to react.

- If we mistake a moral idea for a functional one, we are more likely to misunderstand the implications of the claim.

- We must not make the mistake of confusing one kind of claim with another – whether in our own claims or claims of others.

CHAPTER 4

CLAIMS

Now that we have the emotion/reason distinction under our belts, we will turn to examining the structure of ideas - which will ultimately enable us to take apart ideas for serious analysis. By first getting an understanding of emotion and reason, we have laid the groundwork for better understanding this section. As you read, think about how the structure of arguments changes when we are acting based on reason and on emotion. Think about your own experiences in presenting ideas in different ways; what strategies worked best for you and why?

Throughout this text, we will be using the term "claim" quite a bit. Let's understand what we mean exactly by that term, and why it is important.

A claim is an assertion [a statement] that something is the case. A claim may be positive, meaning that it tells you that something is true. A claim can also be negative, meaning that it tells you that something is false.

A claim may be as simple as "it is true," or as complex as you wish to make it. Sometimes, claims are very convoluted (messy, with a whole lot of different parts that are not clearly connected). However, every claim is ultimately just an assertion (positive or negative) that something is the case i.e. something is true or false.

Here's a simplified way of looking at it: (x) is True or False.

You may be wondering about claims that look a bit different. For example, "football is a sport" is a claim. We can understand this as, "*(football is a sport) is true.*" So, the whole statement is either true or false because it can be subject to **justification(s),** some kind of evidence that the claim is accurate. In other words, given the definitions of "sport" and "football," you can investigate the relationship between the two; in this case, whether football is, in fact, a sport. To do so, you would do an analysis of football, of sport, and then decide whether that statement, as a whole, is true or false. It gets more complicated, and if you'd like to learn more about logic that is at the root of such representations, you can find an amazing free resource through the Open Learning Initiative [13] However, we'll stop with the use of formal logic at this point. All we need to know, for the moment, is that all claims follow this model.

A claim may be given with or without justification. Sometimes, the justification is missing because it seems obvious what the justification is and that the justification is also true. If you're standing outside in the middle of the day, you generally don't have to justify why you think it is daytime. You *could* justify it, but it seems a bit silly to have to prove to someone that, in the middle of the day, it is actually day. Although, if someone asked you why you thought it was daytime, you would have a clear explanation for the justification of your claim. Other times, the lack of justification can seriously weaken a claim because it is unclear what the evidence should be and whether the justification is true. The justification is ultimately what leads a person to make a claim - whether or not a justification is provided, whether or not the justification is a good one. Visually, we can imagine a pyramid whose very top is the claim itself – resting on the justification below.

---

13   Carnegie Mellon University - Open Learning Initiative. *Logic and Proofs*. https://oli.cmu.edu/courses/logic-proofs-copy/

Validity:

Anyone can claim anything. Great! But we're interested in figuring out if the claim "works." So, what does it mean for a claim to work? Well, the justification part of the claim is set up like a series of instructions for assembling furniture: if you do it right and follow the instructions, your product should match the picture on the box. But if the instructions are bad (or you don't follow directions), you end up with something else – usually an unusable mess.

A claim that works is a claim where the instructions of the justification give you the correct product. When the instructions give you the correct final product, we call that a **valid** claim. Validity is a term that has some technical meanings in formal logic, but the definition we'll use for it is this:

A claim is valid if, and only if, it follows from the argument; if the conclusion (claim) is in fact supported by the argument (justification).

Using the visual above, a valid claim is one that has a stable pyramid under it, holding it up. But simply having a pyramid and a top does not mean that you have a valid claim. Here's a simple example:

- Bob: Today is Tuesday.

- You: How do you know that today is Tuesday?

- Bob: Because:

  - 2+2= 4,

- In 1492 Columbus sailed the Ocean Blue, and

- You can't lick your elbow.

- Therefore, it is Tuesday

What's wrong with that justification? A lot. The key part is that it is unrelated to the claim. That is, the claim does not follow from the justification. Visually, you have something like this:

Sure, there is a claim and justification, but unless that justification actually holds up the claim, it might as well not exist.

Things get a bit messier, though, because it turns out that the "stones" that make up your pyramid are usually themselves mini-claims. That is, each of them also has to be valid for the final claim to work. And you can, and sometimes should, go in and check each stone of the pyramid, to make sure the whole thing is actually standing. Here's an example you might have some experience with from your math classes:

$4+6 = ?$

The answer is 10. Yay! We got it right. And if we started with 4 and 6 as givens (that is, the problem asked us to add up 4 and 6), that would be fine. However, imagine if we started with something like this:

- $A+B = ?$

- $A = 2+2$

- B = 17-8

What we get is: A = 4, B = 9.

And then, 4+9 = ?

But now the first equation we had (4+6) is wrong. We're not supposed to be adding up 4+6, and now our answer (10) is wrong. It is wrong because one of our justifications was not valid; because 17-8 is not 6. If you looked only at the final step (4+6 = ?), then 10 is the right answer. That is, the conclusion (10) is valid. But if you dig a bit deeper, you find out that the whole final step (4+6) is wrong. Even though the conclusion drawn from your final step is valid, the final step as a whole is not valid – so your conclusion has to be invalid because your pyramid is broken.

Visually, that looks something like this:

That mess isn't going to support anything. Although we will come back and examine these processes in depth later on, the idea of what a valid claim is should be noted up-front so that there is the least risk of misunderstanding as we go on.

When we find a claim that is not fully supported, whose justification is weak (the justification is not strong enough to hold the weight of the conclusion), or is completely unsupported - we have a bad claim. In fact, this is what makes a bad claim bad. You are very unlikely to have a bad claim with a good justification. Since the justification is the structure holding up the claim, a badly constructed structure means that the claim will collapse. A major problem, however, is being able to distinguish between good and bad justifications. In the next chapter, we will take a look at several problems with claims and justifications, which will help us to clear up some of the confusion.

SUMMARY

- A claim is a statement that something is the case.

- A claim is of the form: X is True/False

- A claim must have a justification – reason for believing it – although the obvious ones might not always be provided.

- A claim is valid if it follows from the argument; if the conclusion (claim) is supported by the argument (justification).

- To check the validity of an argument, we have to make sure the justification (the pyramid) actually works as advertised, and that the claim is actually fully supported by the justification.

- Any claim that is not fully supported, or if the justification is weak, is a bad claim.

CHAPTER 5

PROBLEMS

Now that we have explored how to be rational, stable, and calm, and we know what claims and validity are all about, we are going to turn our attention to claims – how they do and don't work, why, and what to keep an eye out for.

As we approach the issue of analyzing claims, we first have to fully identify the problem before us. You can think of this as a full explanation of why it is important to use critical thinking to carefully examine the claims and justifications we are given. Understanding these problems will help us navigate around them, and not get caught up in bad ideas. It should also help you to not make the same mistakes yourself.

We are faced with an ever-increasing number of claims every day, from all sides. Social media, mainstream media, authoritative sources, experts, etc. are all pumping out so many papers, articles, and media appearances, that it is impossible to keep up with all of them. At the same time, a great deal of these claims are factually and demonstrably garbage. The problem for us, is the fact that their lack of validity does not seem to prevent everyone – from the general public. Doctors, Wall Street investors, and everyone else – from believing these garbage claims, and then presenting them as true.

This **<u>reaction</u>** should not surprise us: emotionally unstable people do have a tendency of running about like headless chickens. That means that our job is to keep our heads, keep calm, and pay close attention to what's going on. It should be noted that you are not alone in facing this problem. Medicine, psychology, hard sciences, etc. are all facing the exact same issue, and generally for the exact same reasons.

So, why do we have so many bad claims?

The Birds and the Bees of Bad Claims

There are a lot of reasons why bad claims get made, pushed forward, and repeated. Here, we will take a look at six major causes of bad claims. While we are presenting these as separate causes, in reality they are often intertwined, so that you have multiple causes at once. Additionally, there are other causes that may also play part in this mess. However, we'll be focusing on these six, because they tend to come up a lot.

As a general rule, people will believe something because A) they want it to be true (they are unreasonably hopeful about a positive outcome), or B) they are afraid that it is true (they are terrified of something, so they act as if their worst fears are about to happen). This is a big part of why people accept claims uncritically: the claim either supports their side so they want it to be true, or it presents some kind of a serious threat they are afraid of. On the other hand, laziness also plays part in accepting claims - we like to be comfortable, and so we accept whatever supports the ideas we already have, and reject whatever would require that we change our thinking. Either way, however, this approach is focused on emotion, not reason.

To a certain extent, the fear and hope is understandable, psychologically speaking. It turns out that being mildly paranoid is good for your survival. Why? If you assume that every strange sound in the forest is a bear coming to kill you and feast on your carcass, you will end up running away from bunnies. However, since you're running from everything, you will also avoid the bears. Similarly, the "hope it's true" position gives us the will to power through some very bad situations.

That said, since we're not in a hunter-gatherer mode, and these decisions can have long-term effects on us, and everyone around us, it is imperative that we actually discern what is going on. We can't afford to flee from all the bunnies, nor can we afford wishful thinking. The following six points will illustrate where a lot of our problems come from, and that will give us a way to rationally engage in responses, instead of emotional reactions.

Publish or Perish

The first culprit of bad claims is a problem called "publish or perish." This refers to the idea that, for many people, the ability to get or maintain a job is based on the continuous publication of their findings in high-profile places. If you are a biologist, that high-profile place is the *Journal of Nature*, or *Science*. If you're a tech-journalist, that high-profile place may be *New York Times* or *Bloomberg News*. If you are a cyber-security analyst, then the location of the publication may be different – but the same principle applies. If you do not have X number of published papers annually, your job is on the line – or at least your annual bonus.

The problem, of course, is that no one's research is that interesting. Meaning, there is no way for these experts to write that many articles of that caliber, based on their actual research and verified claims. At the same time, they need the publications to get ahead. So, people fudge the numbers, sexy-up the conclusions, tweak the data, and get published. Meanwhile, the rest of us end up with a whole boatload of bad claims which we either wrongly believe, or discover to be wrong, after having to spend time checking.

You might be wondering how it is that bad claims get published in peer-reviewed journals (aren't those supposed to be trustworthy sources?). The answer is simple: p-hacking (very informative videos: Veritasium [14] and Crash Course [15]). It boils down to twisting the information until it does what you need it to do, so you can get published. There's also the fact that often enough, the reviewers do a terribly bad job, so things get published regardless of their quality.

Conclusion? Just because something is published does not mean that it's true – or even that it's not absurd.

---

[14]   Veritasium. *Is Most Published Research Wrong?* https://www.youtube.com/watch?v=42QuXLucH3Q

[15]   CrashCourse. *P-Hacking: Crash Course Statistics #30.* https://www.youtube.com/watch?v=Gx0fAjNHb1M

Expert Knowledge

The second culprit is the lack of expert knowledge. Many of the "experts" that write about any topic are not actual experts. They have some general idea about the field, but they're rarely drawn from actual experts in the field. Add to that the fact that most every field of ideas is rather complex and resists easy understanding by the average Joe, and you have a great recipe for misinformation. And this is also true of the media experts that get called in once a story goes viral.

Case in point, when the Equifax hack[16] happened in 2017, one of the many experts on NPR claimed that the stolen Social Security numbers could be used to file fake tax returns. The problem is that this specific scam has been impossible for about a decade - ever since the IRS began to require previous tax data to allow a new filing. The "expert" spoke about the way the Social Security numbers could be exploited **in the past**, but did not mention how the system had changed - or the consequences of that change - and so proceeded to badly misinform the American public about the kind of threat they faced. Either he intentionally lied, or he is entirely incompetent - not sure which is worse.

You might be wondering how "experts" can make such mistakes? Because often enough, the "experts" are really just relatively charismatic people (or people with good enough writing skills) and a decent agent. Well, there is more to it, but that's the quick and dirty version. Think back to the last election or three. How many "experts" had entirely wrong predictions? And these were the "good ones" who were given airtime on national news or columns in major publications.

All too often, you can just call yourself an expert, put whatever you want on a resume, learn some jargon, and there you go. Open up a company that does this "expert" thing, make a decent website, and you're off to the races. Who actually checks your resume? Did you know that, in 2004, at least three National Nuclear Security Administration employees (with top-secret security clearance and "emergency operations responsibilities") had fake diplomas?[17]

Conclusion? The fact that an "expert" said it is not enough to count the claim as true, nor to take it on faith.

---

16   C-Net. *How the Equifax hack happened, and what still needs to be done.* https://www.cnet.com/tech/services-and-software/equifaxs-hack-one-year-later-a-look-back-at-how-it-happened-and-whats-changed/

17   Wired. *U.S. Officials Spot Fake Degrees.* https://www.wired.com/2004/05/u-s-officials-sport-fake-degrees/

Bad Foundation

Third, we have the problem of building on bad information. Once a bad claim makes its way into the general consciousness, it infects the rest of our knowledge. That means, as we work to understand later issues, the bad batch of information from before keeps tainting our new work product.

Case in point, the popular show *24* was big on the idea of torture as a very effective tool for gathering information (and as a popular show, it spread the idea widely). Of course, we are all aware that the show in question is fiction. Yet, despite that knowledge, in 2007 Supreme Court Justice Scalia[18] insisted that torture could be a highly effective way of gathering information from terror suspects – citing *24* as the source of his beliefs. That would be bad enough, but now we have access to the 2014 CIA torture report that concluded that the use of torture to extract information has not produced any meaningful information. And yet, in 2017, President Donald Trump[19] still pushed the idea that torture works. That's the problem of bad claims tainting later information. And if it can happen at the highest levels of our government, it's safe to say that other parts of our society are susceptible to that problem as well.

Take, for example, the aforementioned p-hacking. One bad study gets out there, and it is then picked up by others, who assume it to be true – because it was published. They then use that study as a premise for further ideas – which might also end up getting p-hacked – and now you have layers of terrible and published ideas that are starting to permeate the social fabric.

The anti-vaxxers had one study, and that one was retracted because it was a garbage study at all levels.[20] However, once it went viral (pun intended), there was no putting that genie back in the bottle. And now, we have a proliferation of anti-vaxxers and a return of the Measles.

Conclusion? One bad claim tends to create another; always check the underlying premises for a garbage foundation.

---

18   The Atlantic. *Scalia and Torture.* https://www.theatlantic.com/daily-dish/archive/2007/06/scalia-and-torture/227548/

19   CNN. *Donald Trump says torture "absolutely works" - but does it?* https://www.cnn.com/2017/01/26/politics/donald-trump-torture-waterboarding/index.html

20   Nature. *The discredited doctor hailed by the anti-vaccine movement.* https://www.nature.com/articles/d41586-020-02989-9

Authoritative Sources

Fourth, is the issue of authoritative sources. Authoritative sources are the expert individuals, professional organizations, peer-reviewed journals, etc. We've already noted some problems with experts and publications, but there is much more to be considered.

What authoritative sources do for us, or what they're supposed to do, is outsource the need for our verification of the claim. This is an old concept with roots in the very idea of work specialization. When your plumbing goes bad, you call a plumber. When your roof is leaking, you call a roofer. Why? Because their expertise in the specific task should make them **more capable of solving the problem** than the average Joe. That's why you go to a doctor when you're sick – because they presumably know more about illness and health than you do.

This outsourcing is intended as a time-saving effort, and one that increases the likelihood of a better outcome. It is timesaving, because it means that you don't have to go and learn how to do every job you need done. Instead, you hire an expert – i.e. an authoritative source of problem-solving for the field. Similarly, doctors do not research every new drug that shows up; instead, they rely on the FDA and the research published on the drug, to decide whether to prescribe it to a patient. However, with the proliferation of the "experts," a flood of papers and claims, and quality decline in the expertise of the authority, the authoritative sources are no more secure from publishing or endorsing bad claims than anyone else.

Imagine doing math. Doing it by hand is tedious, and you may make a mistake. A calculator is a tool that outsources the process and is mechanized (just push buttons in the correct order). It increases the likelihood of a correct answer, does the job faster, etc., and it only needs a bit of tool-use training to do its job. Now, imagine that the calculator gave you the wrong answer 30% of the time. It is no longer a timesaving tool that increases your likelihood of being correct. Now it is a positive liability.

This has become the case with authoritative sources. Top medical journals publish deeply flawed and flat-out incorrect papers. Only 6 out of the 53-basic science studies looking at potential treatment targets in cancer are replicable. That means that 47 peer-reviewed, published, cancer treatment targets used by your doctor, don't do anything.[21] Drug-testing for FDA (Food and Drug Administration) approval

---

21   TED. *What doctor don't know about the drugs they prescribe | Ben Goldacre.* https://www.youtube.com/

allows the companies to selectively publish their results for the purpose of the approval. So, for antidepressants,[22] 47 positive and 3 negative results were published to the FDA, and that's how the FDA gave their approval for antidepressants to be available on the market. But, in fact, there were 97 trials total, of which **49 were negative** and 48 positive. The companies making anti-depressants *hid half of their results*, so it looked like they essentially only had positive results. The FDA relies on the data the companies give them to accept or reject the drug; and your doctor relies on the FDA to prescribe medicine to you.

This is not a problem just for medicine. Psychology can't replicate nearly 50% of its published claims. Yet, these ideas are still out there, because once they enter the popular consciousness, they are rather difficult to dislodge. A bombastic headline today sells newspapers today (or gets clicks, etc.). And if you're wrong, tomorrow you publish a retraction on page 17, in font 4. For most authoritative sources, there is no cost to being wrong; only a cost to not publishing.

It should be noted that, within authoritative institutions, the publish-or-perish ideology is in full force. That, and incentivization for clicks is also very much present. I happened to overhear the author of a much quoted (yet complete garbage) paper remark, "*If I get another publication in* [certain field] *this year, I get a bonus.*" Note, he needs a publication, not factual claims.

Conclusion? Authoritative sources are not as authoritative as you think. The mere fact that they push something does not make it true or functional.

Profit Motive

We should also note here the profit motive as a separate, fifth, category. Although publications in a publish-or-perish system are already a profit motive in their own right, they are not the only kind of profit motive.

Service providers, for example, rely on the perceived need for their product to stay afloat. That is, they need to ensure that the particular problem is one you are worried about enough to hire outside help, and they need to ensure that you perceive them as the best source of such help. Think of all those "as seen

---

watch?v=RKmxL8VYy0M

22   *Ibid.*

on TV" commercials, where apparently peeling a potato is an existential threat.[23] The idea is to present a problem, make it important enough for you to get outside help (product), and make it enticing enough ("But wait! There's more!"). When a security vendor – like the people selling you anti-virus software or home security systems – is explaining the threat and their own capabilities, what you are witnessing is profit-motive at work. The presentation is, ultimately, a sales-pitch. Therefore, they have all the incentive to make you feel as if the Armageddon is upon you, and they are the only way to save yourself.

Conclusion? When your money is the goal of those providing you with information, the only reasonable assumption is that they have all the reason to also be engaged in deception (intentionally or by relying on ultimately bad claims) to ensure that you are parted from your cash.

<u>Statistics</u>

Sixth, and last for now, let's talk about statistics. You may have heard the old adage: *there are lies, there are damned lies, and then there are statistics.*

Statistics present a rather sizable problem. Part of the reason is that they are quite often derived in incredibly faulty ways. So faulty, in fact, that they carry all the factual weight of tween fan fiction. From sample-size, to sample type, to the kinds of questions asked, kinds of data collected, connections drawn, etc. statistics are too often unreliable to begin with.

Yet, even when the statistics are collected in a well-designed way, they pose a problem. The fact of the matter is, we can twist statistics in any way we want. A mere change in perspective gives us an entirely different picture. That is, without changing the data, without doing anything otherwise impermissible, a slightly different angle gives us a whole new picture.

For example, the claims of sexism in the pay difference between men and women US National Soccer teams, is based on verified numbers that each is paid. Without getting into the issue of pay disparity, let's see how the same stats can get turned around. Women make $37,000, while men make $71,000 as their base National Team salary. From this perspective (total dollar amount), men get paid more than women. However, the average female player also makes base $37,000 annually by playing for the private

---

23   Potato Peeling Gloves. https://www.youtube.com/watch?v=C6r7edRmXl0&t=40s

club (i.e. working). Therefore, the national team pays the women 100% of their club salary (matches it). The average male player makes base $2,000,000+ annually playing for their club. Therefore, the national team pays the men 3.5% of their club salary. From that perspective (percent of base salary), men get paid 96.5% less than women (in terms of matching the salary) – despite being paid more in terms of a simple dollar amount. Same statistics, different results.

Women average base salary (club)	**$37,000**
Women National Team salary	**$37,000**
National Team pay as percent of base salary	**100%**
Men average base salary (club)	**$2,000,000**
Men National Team salary	**$71,000**
National Team pay as percent of base salary	**3.55%**

Statistics can be used to prove just about anything you want. And you can collect them in just about any way you want. The mere publication of stats does not mean anything. In fact, even when they are revealed as entirely faulty, statistics persist, and they are built upon in later research – providing an ever-deeper hole of bad claims we seem to be drowning in.

Conclusion? You should assume that statistics prove nothing – generally speaking. It's only when you can see what's actually being compared to what, and how, and why, that you might be able to make some use of that information – and even then, on the assumption that the collection of the data, the size of the dataset, etc. are actually functional.

CONCLUSION

What these issues lead us to is the following conclusion: **trust no one!**

As claims are put forward, we can no longer hope that the outsourcing to experts etc. will be enough to weed out the garbage. That job is once again falling to us. Perhaps, one day, we can rebuild the authoritative institutions – but for now, all this work falls to us. We have to move away from outsourcing the processes of critical thinking. We have to understand the problems and pitfalls already here, and we have to learn how to properly think about the problems and solutions. Hoping that *Steve the blogger* will do so for us is incoherent, given that Steve is there to make money and that click-bait and proliferation of bombastic claims is far more financially lucrative for the Steves of the world.

SUMMARY

There are a whole host of reasons why bad claims get published, pushed, and repeated.

- Publish or perish incentivizes people to misrepresent their research, to publish it, and stay in business.

- Expert knowledge is often very lacking., Instead of informing, it tends to misinform us.

- Bad foundation, laid by faulty publications and bad expertise, creates a sense of knowing (in both expert and the general populations), which then produces new, faulty ideas based off of bad claims.

- Authoritative sources, which become a way for us to outsource thinking, turn out to be just as iffy as everything else – except that everyone believes their bad claims.

- Profit motive leads people to do anything for their personal benefit. And because bad claims are an easy way to get noticed, published, etc. it often plays a part of that process.

- Statistics misinform more often than not, because you can do almost anything with them; and you can create them however you feel like. In reality, while statistics do give us some information, it's the use and interpretation of that information that is the key.

CHAPTER 6

THE ISSUE OF INTERPRETATION

We explained the idea of claims, justification and validity in chapter 4, and followed it up with the kinds of problems that arise (most often on the justification side) in chapter 5. In this chapter, we will examine the role of **interpretation** in understanding claims and justifications. Interpretation matters, because the facts never actually speak for themselves; we give them meaning by interpreting them (that is, we use our own models for understanding the world to make sense of the facts). This is why just throwing facts at the other person never wins an argument; the same facts can be interpreted differently by different people. To make sure that the justifications and claims make sense, we have to understand how to properly interpret them.

Interpreting Facts

The first thing to note is that facts are meaningless. I don't mean that facts are unimportant. Instead, facts, as facts, do not have any meaning. What gives facts meaning is the act of interpretation.

Interpretation is how we order facts and how we relate them to each other and to ourselves. Let's clarify this through a simple example:

Let's say that Tesla stock dropped by 50% today. That's a fact (a made-up fact for this example, but let's call it a fact). If you have never heard of Tesla, this fact means nothing to you. If your life savings are invested in Tesla stock, this means that you just lost a half of your life savings. If you're 20 and you lost half your life savings, that means one thing. If you are retiring tomorrow and you lost half of your life savings, that means something else entirely. If you did a short-sale of Tesla stock yesterday, this fact means that you just made a lot of money. The fact is the same in every case. However, its meaning is not in the fact, but in the interpretation – and that interpretation depends on you.

You can also think of it this way: if the meaning of the fact was in the fact itself, we would all have the same understanding of what a fact means. But the same fact that brings joy to Bob, brings you grief (let's say that Bob stole your car). So, the meaning of the fact is never in the fact, but in the interpretation you give it.

About 55 million people die every year.[24] That's a fact. But how many of those mean anything to you? How many do you cry over? Usually, you cry for 0/55,000,000 per year. Why? Because they are strangers you know nothing about, which have no impact on you, and whose passing you don't even notice. But when it's your grandmother who passed away, you most certainly notice. That death is meaningful to you. The fact that people die is – effectively – irrelevant, unless the fact is in a proper kind of relation to you. At that point, it can shatter your whole world.

The facts we get are often the same, but how we interpret them ultimately ends up governing our course of action - i.e. how we use our "understanding" of said facts. In order to properly analyze a claim, you have to understand the meaning of the relevant facts *for the person making the claim,* and the way that the meaning bears on the interpretation they are offering. We also have to understand what those facts mean to us, so that we can avoid an emotional reaction to a potentially justified claim.

---

24   Our World in Data. *How Many People Die and How Many are Born Each Year?* https://ourworldindata.org/births-and-deaths

Interpretive Models

What we mean when we say "interpretation" is actually a model for creating **relations** between the various facts and groups of facts, for assigning particular **values** to certain ideas, for placing and removing **emphasis** from particular areas, for including and excluding ideas and facts on the basis of perceived **relevance**, and for deriving a **meaning** in a way that gives you something like an understanding of the world. **Interpretative models are the lens through which we order facts and relate them to each other and to ourselves.** You may have noticed that, in debates, we very rarely disagree on facts. What we disagree on is the meaning of those facts. And after all the "debating," no one has changed their mind, because their interpretation of the facts has not been changed by naming more facts.

Case in point, the question of emphasis (where you put the stress in a claim) is at the root of the disagreement about the second amendment.

> A well regulated Militia, being necessary to the security of a free State, the right of the people to keep and bear Arms, shall not be infringed.[25]

Should the emphasis be on a *well-regulated militia*, or on the *right to bear arms*? Scholars on both sides of the argument point to the original text – the same facts – yet the difference in their models for understanding the world cause them to place the emphasis on a different element of that fact – and thus, the whole disagreement.

All models are inherently based on axioms. **Axioms are starting assumptions and definitions that are not subject to justification**; they are simply taken as starting points we assume to be the truth that cannot be questioned.[26] In math, things like definitions of triangles, etc. are axiomatic. You don't have to justify why a triangle has three sides, and so on. For example, how do I know that reason is reasonable - that reason actually works? I could try to prove or demonstrate that reason works, but I immediately run

---

25   U.S. Constitution. Second Amendment. https://constitution.congress.gov/constitution/amendment-2/

26   Kant famously demonstrates the inability to prove or disprove such axioms in his *Four Antinomies*; while Asimov (*Reason*) succinctly summarizes this issue as, "You can prove anything you want by coldly logical reason – if you pick the proper postulates… [but] postulates are based on assumption and adhered to by faith. Nothing in the Universe can shake them."

into a problem: *proof, demonstration, argument, etc. are all things that rely on using reason.* That means that the only way to prove that reason works, is by first *assuming that reason works* (otherwise, there is no reason to accept the proof). So, the assumption that reason is reasonable is axiomatic; it does not require justification, because it is impossible to give a justification. I have to assume this to be true, and go from there. That assumption is necessary for me to make sense of the world, to know how to act, etc.

Axioms are the lens through which we create our interpretive models of the world. They tell us about the kinds of direction that will be used to interpret all facts.

If the axiom is, say, that Mongolia is a grave threat to the U.S. democracy, then all data will be interpreted to lead to that conclusion. Data that is contrary to that axiom will either be disregarded as somehow false, or it will be interpreted in a way (no matter how unlikely) that essentially points to the grave threat Mongolia represents. If Mongolia agrees to some demand we place on them, the agreement will not be a sign of improving relations, it's "just what Mongolia wants, so they can lull you into a false sense of security."

A great example of this axiomatic core, and the way it interprets facts, is conspiracy theories. Once you accept the idea that the government is run by a secret cabal, bent on... whatever, you can interpret everything that happens as part of that axiomatic belief (see: Reptilian Conspiracy)[27]. The interpretive model of the Reptilian Conspiracy is the lens through which some people interpret the world - and then, everything comes up reptilians. That means that the claims coming from such sources do not have to be factually wrong in order to be a perverted interpretation of the truth – at least according to your own interpretive model.

Bias

This brings us to the next point: **all data is biased**. I don't mean that the individual facts are biased (2+2 = 4 is not biased), but rather that the aggregation of individual facts into "data" is inherently biased by our interpretive models. This is because, when you are collecting facts, you are always focused on what you perceive to be **relevant** facts, and exclude all those things that you consider to be irrelevant.

---

27   Wikipedia. *Reptilian Conspiracy Theory*. https://en.wikipedia.org/wiki/Reptilian_conspiracy_theory

You do this out of necessity, because there is an infinite number of facts available in the world, but most of them are probably not useful to your idea.

The last time you lost internet connection, did you check the router? Yes. That's the assumption of relevance at work. Did you check the position of Venus, relative to Jupiter? No. Why not? Because you made the *assumption* that such data was not relevant to your problem. Why? Because your interpretive model told you so.

While astrology seems like a funny way to prove a point, the principle is the same wherever you go. Has there been a time when your interpretation failed to account for something that turned out to be relevant? Of course there has. Has there been a time when your interpretation included things that turned out to be irrelevant? Of course there has. That is the proof of the fact that data is biased. It is biased in your relevance-based collection, it's biased in your assumptions of proper emphasis, etc. This is not a problem you can do away with, it is a feature of thinking you must account for.

It is important to understand that, in terms of biased data, it's not just you or me who have to deal with it. Everyone, in every field, is dealing with the exact same problem. It is part of what it means to be human. Pick a field, any field. Physics has included a lot of data that turned out to be irrelevant, and excluded a lot of important data. So has psychology, social sciences, history, and every other academic discipline ever - not to mention your private life. The only way to not have this problem is to already know everything that can ever possibly be known on the subject. That way, you know in advance what matters and what does not.

"Knowing everything" has a term – *omniscience*. That term is generally reserved for monotheistic definitions of God – as in: "all knowing, all seeing," etc. Since we can safely assume that you, I, and any given expert is not actually God Almighty, we can assume that we don't have omniscience. And so, biased data is just a thing we have to deal with and account for.

Interpretation

Finally, we are faced with a third issue: **there are an infinite number of ways to interpret the exact same data**. We know this, because facts do not have meaning on their own and must be interpreted.

Interpretation is not part of the facts, and depends only on one's starting axioms and the way we develop them. We can have any interpretation of the world you like - including the noted Reptilian Conspiracy interpretation.

Take, for example, the people reading this text. There are a finite number of people, and therefore a finite number of features they may have - this is data. Yet, we can divide the data up in an infinite number of ways. That is, we can *interpret* the reader data in infinite ways. We can divide readers up by age, race, ethnicity, height, weight, eye color, hair color, astrological sign, shoe size, preferred shirt-type, favorite drink, number of cells currently undergoing mitosis in their bodies, etc. To get really funky, run an intersectionality model on that data.[28] With every new feature you get an exponential rise in groups. Same data, infinite parsing options.

Why does this matter? Because the meaninglessness of facts, bias of data, and infinite interpretation potential are used to create bad claims, and then to hide the fact that they have no real value. Quite often, the very reason why bad claims manage to take off and persist is because their failings are hidden in the way they are assembled. In order to cut through the illusion of such claims, we need to be aware of the kinds of subtle issues that are at play.

This situation appears dire. However, it does not mean that all interpretations are equal, or that there is nothing else to be done. What we are really interested in is the idea of functionality.

Functionality

Functionality is the degree to which the interpretive model provides coherent, *explanatory*, and *actionable* conclusions – for our purposes.

Let's take a look at these three features.

Coherence means that the system is rational – that it holds together. In a coherent system, you

---

28   Intersectionality is what you get when the number of features you are interested in are further expanded by stacking. So that, if you only have two features (say, A and B), you can end up with intersectional features AA, AB, BA, and BB. The total number of intersectional features you end up with is the number of initial features (X) raised to the power of the number of initial features (X^X). With 2 features (like A, B) you have 2^2 intersectional features (4 total). With three features, you have 3^3 intersectional features (27 total). By the time you get to just 7 features, you have a staggering 823,543 possible intersectional features!

have something like known causes for known effects, stable relations between different features, etc. A coherent system is needed, because an incoherent system is pure chaos. You can't do anything with chaos, because you have no idea what anything means. The thing that ends up having a great result today could be the thing that kills you tomorrow: there is no rhyme or reason. All the parts of a coherent system fit together without contradiction; incoherent systems contradict themselves.

Building on the coherence requirement, we have the "explanatory" feature. For an interpretation to be explanatory, it must – no surprise here – be able to explain how and why certain outcomes happen. This allows us to then track what kinds of results we can expect from different inputs - different possible actions. This is something like the relation between the justification and the claim: if you have a great justification, but it is not connected to your claim, then it does not justify anything.

Finally, the actionable requirement tells us that we're supposed to be able to use the coherent and explanatory feature to **do something**. If I can understand the system, and it gives me explanations as to how and why things happen, I also must be able to do something with that information, or else I just have a description of the world. Descriptions are great, but what I need is a way of making use of them to do other things.

For example, while people are perfectly free to claim that, "Zeus governs the success you will have on your math exam," that is not a functional model for us – because I can't do a single thing with that model of interpretation. I need something that will give me a coherent understanding of the process, that will explain both what is happening and why, and that will allow me to do something about it. The will of Zeus does not meet those criteria, so it becomes non-functional.

Functionality is a key feature of looking at claims. Functionality is about how practical the claim is, and the justification for that claim, for *me and for my ideas.*

Let's say I decide to buy everyone reading this book a pair of flip-flops. And, to be thorough in the flip-flop ordering, I get everyone's feet precisely measured by some kind of a laser-guided foot-measuring device. Now, I can make sure that the flip-flops I send you are absolutely perfect for your feet. That's great.

Now, let's say that next week I want to buy all of you your favorite Starbucks drink. I still have the data for your foot size. Can I use it? Well, I could, but it would be pointless. Why? Because the foot-size data is **not functional for my purposes**. This is important: just because someone has done a study, or they collected data, does not mean that this information is of any use at all to me. To be useful to me, the data needs to be functional for me and for my purposes.

This is part of why we can't just rely on the fact that something got published. It matters quite a bit what got published, what is and is not included in that data set, and how it is and is not interpreted. Unless **those features** match what I am working on, all the data in the world is simply useless to me.

There is an additional way we can understand the *"coherent, explanatory,* and *actionable* conclusions"* definition of functionality - and one that I think is rather useful - through internal coherence and external coherence.

Internal coherence (part of the "coherent" feature of functionality) is a matter of whether the claim works according to the system the author presents it in. If I give you several statements that are supposed to be true, but they contradict each other in a way that I can't resolve, then I have an internally incoherent claim. Here are some examples:

Let's say we have an argument based on three equations:

1. $3x = 21$ ($x = 7$)

2. $4y = 16$ ($y = 4$)

3. $x = y$

Each of those equations makes sense on its own. Additionally, Equation 1 and 3 make sense together, 2 and 3 make sense together, and 1 and 2 make sense together. But when you try to put all three of them together, you end up with a problem: $7 = 4$ is just not possible. That is internal incoherence.

Another way to think of this is in terms of movies. A *plot hole* in a movie is a problem of internal coherence. If the hobbits are rescued by Iron-Man, the issue is that the world described by the film has violated its own rules (unless you are doing a mash-up comedy - which would be a way to resolve the apparent contradiction).

On the other hand, the fact that there are no dragons, hobbits, or Iron-Man in the real world is not a plot hole, i.e. it is not an issue of coherence internal to the film. It does not matter for internal coherence that the features described are not real. We only care whether they create a description of the world that does not contradict itself.

Similarly, the coherence of the functionality of the claim is all about whether the claim works by its own definitions. The only part we care about here is whether the claim has parts that contradict each other in a way that we can't somehow do away with.

External coherence (part of the "explanatory" and "actionable" feature of functionality) asks whether an idea works when compared to our own understanding of reality. If I give you several statements that are supposed to be true, and they don't contradict each other, but they still **don't work**, then I have an externally incoherent claim.

External coherence is a question of whether the proposed idea works in reality, i.e. in the world we happen to be in. Here, the fact that there are no dragons, elves, or Iron-Man is important, because we need to know how things work and how to act. If we assume that Iron-Man will solve our problems, and Iron-Man is not real, then we are in for a rather nasty surprise. If internal coherence is an issue of "plot holes" in movies, then external coherence is an issue of "reality holes" in our lives.

The actionability of functionality of the claim is all about whether we can use that claim when we apply it to the real world. We can apply anything where the results will be what we predicted them to be. For example, Romans believed that malaria was caused by stale air. As a result, they built their cities and forts away from smelly places - like swamps. The result was fewer malaria cases. Notice that the fact that "bad air" is not really the cause of malaria did not prevent their claim from being actionable. That is, if I acted out their solution to the malaria problem, I got the desired results - even though their explanation may have been wrong.

Additionally, the external coherence of a claim is accompanied by a justification for why this particular action is supposed to work, rather than any other, and that gives us our **explanatory** feature of functionality.

A claim that is not internally coherent cannot, by definition, be externally coherent (it is impossible for irrational ideas to be real). A claim that is internally coherent **may** be externally coherent, but is not necessarily so (think: a well-written alternate history novel – e.g. *Abraham Lincoln: Vampire Hunter*). The ability to properly explore and evaluate the interpretive model, as well as any claims in that model, and to apply the internal and external coherence tests, is critical to understanding the ultimate validity of a claim, and is at the heart of good analysis of the claim.

The focus on functionality through internal and external coherence, gives us a great way to both understand the interpretive models of others - as well as understanding whether any particular claim or justification is functional for our purposes. The mapping that is required to make sure the internal coherence of a claim works is also a very useful feature of much of our later ideas.

This brings us to the end of our second section. We have examined what claims are and how they're structured and some common problems with claims and their justification. In this chapter, we considered three important features to understanding claims, and how the idea of functionality allows us to navigate these features. Putting it all together, we should now understand how claims do and don't work, common problems, and the ways to identify and avoid them. If we put it all together with the first section, we can now see how taking the rational approach protects us from bad claims, by taking a step back and responding (rather than reacting) to claims. When we begin to respond, we are forced to face the question of interpretation, functionality, and claim validity - which then gives us a better starting point for understanding what is actually going on.

In the next section, we will turn our attention to context. The role of context is absolutely crucial to any attempt at critical thinking. In that section, we will learn why context matters, how missing context warps ideas, and will learn how to get the context we need by asking the right questions in the right order.

SUMMARY

- Facts are meaningless and depend on something other than facts to make sense of them

- The way we make sense of facts is through interpretive models.

- Interpretive models are a series of often-axiomatic assumptions we have made about how the world is and is not, which then helps us to sort facts according to that model.

  - This is the lens through which we interpret the world and the data.

- All data is biased, because our interpretive models (with their axiomatic assumptions) tell us what is and is not relevant.

  - It turns out that our ideas of what is and is not relevant can be wrong. Therefore, our data is inherently biased. You can't avoid it, but you can account for it.

- We can interpret the exact same data (facts) in an infinite number of ways.

  - This is the case because facts do not tell us how to interpret them; because our interpretation is based on axiomatic assumptions we have about the world; because which facts will be seen as relevant or irrelevant, and how we will place emphasis on those facts, is always biased.

- Because we are concerned with the functionality of claims, we focus on coherent, explanatory, and actionable conclusions of those interpretations – for our purposes.

- A useful way of examining functionality is through internal and external coherence

  - Internal coherence tests whether the ideas behind the claim contradict each other in a way that cannot be resolved.

  - External coherence tests whether the conclusions of the claim will work if we apply them in real life.

- This tells us that we have to understand the interpretive models, data biases, and interpretation type used by those who make the claim (so that we can see whether their approach fits our own understanding of the world) before we can agree or disagree.

CHAPTER 7
CONTEXT

Welcome to section three! In this section, we're looking at the bread and butter of critical thinking: asking the right questions in the right order to get the right context. Now that we already understand that we need to be responding, and we understand how the justification is supposed to support the claim, we will turn our attention to taking apart the claim and the justification, and making sure they actually work functionally. This process can seem somewhat daunting, but once you understand what questions to ask (and why we're asking them), you will see that it is actually fairly simple.

In fact, you might be surprised by how simple the process is, and reasonably wonder if such a simple procedure can actually get you the promised results. That is a fair question. In answer, I like to quote Sun Tzu (the Classical Chinese philosopher who wrote the *Art of War*). At the beginning of that book, Sun Tzu lists the criteria needed for always attaining certain military victories. He then adds:

All commanders are familiar with these criteria, yet it is he who masters them who takes the victory…

What this means is that Sun Tzu's ideas are not about reinventing the wheel. His book (which is still used by all major military academies, some 2,600 years later) is not about new ideas, but about mastering the key ideas about war. In the same way, this book is not about inventing new ways to think critically, but about presenting the key ideas, and giving you a way to master them.

The key idea we must master, in order to master critical thinking, is context.

Context – it's everything! It's everywhere, and without it we miss the point. As an example of context, and by way of getting a solid definition, I like to start by looking at the Oxford English Dictionary (OED) and etymology. This allows us to make sure we're all on the same page.

The OED defines **context** as, "circumstances that form the setting for an event, statement, or idea, and in terms of which it can be fully understood." Etymologically, the word **context** comes from the Latin "contextus," meaning "weave together" – as in textiles (like cloth and rugs). Here, the etymological background is useful, because we see that the idea of context comes from the notion of the "thing" being part of a larger whole, part of a tapestry or backdrop in which the object of interest is found.

Context is the backdrop against which the events, statements, and ideas should be projected, to make sense of them. Everyone's had the experience of entering a room, or a conversation, only to hear the last line of a statement, the punchline of a joke, and be left entirely in the dark. Although we hear the final piece of information, the absence of the rest of it leaves us confused. An easy example is just hearing the line, "…and that's why Hitler was right." This is a good example, because the statement is very dicey – we can't just nod our head in agreement, because we are lacking the context that makes the distinction between supporting genocide or investing in highway infrastructure.[29] Without the appropriate context, we have trouble understanding the point, and getting all the information. Part of the problem comes from not knowing where our attention *should* be focused. If we focus on the wrong part, we easily draw the wrong conclusions. We may become offended, where offense is not a reasonable position. We may agree, where agreement is not reasonable. We may ask unreasonable questions, or fail to ask crucial ones. In short, we may react when we should respond.

---

29   Boingboing. *You know who else invested in infrastructure?*
https://boingboing.net/2017/02/01/you-know-who-else-invested-in.html

This, of course, leads us to the question: how do we find the context? While there is a number of ways to do so, I prefer getting answers to the following six general questions:

1. Who is the speaker?

Knowing the speaker/author allows us insight into their areas of expertise, agenda and motivations, biases, perspectives, etc. These factors help better explain several of the following questions as well. Every speaker is different and they have a different interpretation of the world. Understanding the speaker lets us understand the difference between an academic talk and a late-night TV commercial.

2. Who is the intended audience?

Knowing who is being addressed plays a crucial role in understanding the context. We deal with boards of directors meetings differently than we do with our close friends and family. We have different styles of communication, different degrees of jargon-usage and technical complexity. There are simply things we do not say publicly – which is generally known as *tact*.

Part of this difference comes from the idea that each different audience has a different set of interests, assumptions, social rules, etc. When you are in a business meeting, the relevant information is the part that will allow you to do your job. When we are playing with little children, the relevant information is rather different.

3. What is the content?

You can think of content as the executive summary of the ideas being communicated. When you're looking to summarize information, it's all about the most relevant content. This is why Cliff Notes are a lot shorter than the original text. This is why the phrase TL;DR exists.[30]

Obviously, if we do not have a firm grasp on the content, our ability to understand what is being communicated drops precipitously. Generally, if you cannot summarize the content in 3 sentences or less, you do not have a firm grasp on it. Yes, that includes extremely complicated and long texts - like Tolstoy's *War and Peace*.

---

30   TL:DR means "too long; didn't read."

4. What is the delivery method?

Delivery method is how the content is being communicated. There is a difference between academic papers, sci-fi novels, business press releases, and government press briefings. They might all have the same content, but the way the information is being communicated will differ.

We often confuse content and delivery, and extra care should be exercised to make the distinction. The same content can be communicated across a variety of delivery methods. Here, the definitions of the speaker and audience are also important, as that relation can heavily influence *appropriateness* of the means of communicating the content. For example, Noam Chomsky, the Department of Justice, and Chris Rock may deliver essentially the same content on race relations between the minorities and the police. Their methods of delivery, however, will be very different. If Chris Rock uses the DOJ method, he'll be out of business. If the DOJ uses Chris Rock's method, there will be a public apology and people getting fired. The delivery method also carries a host of connotations about its appropriateness, based on the three previous questions.

We will also take a moment to address a common problem: literal reading. Reading a statement literally (whether you are reading or listening) means that we take the claims explicitly at face value. That is, we assume that every statement is meant as directly true. The problem, of course, is that we rarely ever speak in such literal ways. We use a lot of metaphors, idioms, similes, analogies, sarcasm, and so on. Although we will spend more time on this issue later, it is important to note right away that we must be on the lookout for these non-literal ways of speaking to properly understand both the delivery method and the content.

5. What is the general context?

This is a sizable question, and we will take a look at the specifics in Chapter 9. For now, general context requires us to answer questions like: *who, what, where, when, why, how, what does that mean, etc.?* Some of these overlap with the previous four questions, and some are entirely unique in this category.

For example, the question of *when* is crucial in distinguishing between racist and non-racist speech. The selection of race-related terminology used by Mark Twain, J. F. Kennedy, MLK, James Baldwin, and

Malcom X reflects – in part – the linguistic history of a nation. The terminology these speakers used in their ideas about race, was the terminology of that moment in the development of language and terminology in their very specific context. We must understand those features of their language in order to understand the content they are communicating. In the same way, we must understand the features of Shakespearean English (as opposed to modern American English) if we want to actually understand what it is that *Hamlet* is trying to communicate.

6. What is the intent?

This is, perhaps, the most difficult question. Unlike the previous ones, where an objective analysis was applicable, the question of intent resides solely in the mind of the author/speaker. As a result, we have no direct access to the intent. However, this does not prevent us from answering this question entirely. If we can answer the other five questions, the issue of intent generally resolves itself (at least in broad strokes). While we may not have certainty, we can have high confidence in the answer we arrive at.

Intent matters, because it allows us to read charitably those statements that may otherwise seem inflammatory or out of place. For example, if you see me get up, go to the kitchen, pour myself a glass of water, and drink it, you can reasonably assume that I had intended to get some water – or at least to get "a drink." We make these kinds of "good enough" calculations of intent all the time, and they are necessary to understand the meaning behind the things we see and hear.

If we cannot answer these 6 questions, we are missing context. Missing the context means that we're seeing only part of the picture. While the parts missing may be irrelevant, it is far more likely that they are absolutely crucial to understanding the claim. The only way to make that determination is by getting the rest of the context, and then making the call.

Let's take a look at a great example of context being everything. We have two images:

Figure 1 *Figure 2*

In both cases, we have a triangular shape, with an open bottom. However, *Figure 1* is the Greek *lambda* (letter "L"). *Figure 2*, on the other hand, is the Chinese character *ren* ("human"). By themselves, the two symbols are very similar – and if your handwriting is anything like mine, the two will look fairly similar on paper. Nothing about their shapes is inherently Greek or Chinese, and nothing about their meaning is given in the shape alone. So, to understand what we're looking at, we need to know the context in which these symbols appear.

But it gets better, or rather, more complex. Even once we know its Greek meaning, the context of *Figure 1* makes the difference between just seeing a letter, feeling safe, and running for your life. This comes from the fact that the Spartan shields featured the *lambda* as a symbol of Spartan military. If those shields are on your side, there is a feeling of safety. If those shields are charging at your position, there is a feeling of existential dread and a need to run for your life. If the letter is printed on a page, then there is no need for either. In this case, context is everything.

The same complexity arises with the character *ren* (*Figure 2*), depending on its usage. You could use it to say something like, "the human was eaten by a tiger," in which case the context is sparse and the meaning direct. But, if we find the term in the *Analects of Confucius*, the connotations of what it means to be human are going to feature very prominently – and so the context again becomes everything.

We'll use one final example: Here is a line of pixels without context.

Take a good look. Take as much time as you'd like.

What is it?

You have no way of knowing, because I removed all the context from the equation. You can subject it to whatever test you'd like, for as long as you'd like, but there is no way of determining what it is. This is exactly what every claim without context looks like. It is ultimately unknowable, because we can't situate it in the proper context.

But, if we just add the context back in, suddenly you know exactly what those pixels are:

In the end, context tells us not just what the rest of the picture is, it informs us about what the original pixels were as well.

Context matters, a lot. Without context, there is no way to understand a claim. As an analogy, if the claim is a punchline of a joke, the context is the setup. Without the setup, you have no idea whether the punchline is funny or not. In fact, you can't even figure out whether what you heard was a punchline or not. For a great bit on this exact problem, I highly suggest looking up the hilarious Lewis Black IHOP <u>sketch</u> (warning: graphic language).[31]

In my classes, I like to demonstrate this point by writing something on the board, in a different (non-English) language or in a different (usually made-up) script, and then asking my students if they agree or disagree with the statement. Suddenly, there isn't a single person who has an opinion one way or another. Why not? Because they are very much aware that they are missing the information necessary to have an opinion. Unfortunately, when it's a language we understand, we also tend to think that we suddenly know all we need to know as well. The only safe approach is to assume that we are ignorant, and collect all the context we can before offering an opinion. The worst that can happen is that you spend a bit of time getting context you already knew. The best case is that you learn something new, and can actually have a coherent idea about what is going on.

---

31   https://youtu.be/73GKhOwhPzs [you can also search for "Lewis Black IHOP horse"]

SUMMARY

- Context is the backdrop against which claims and events should be understood, to make sense of them

  o This is because context is what properly directs our attention, so that we can discover the functional meaning of the claim

- Without context, it is impossible to meaningfully make sense of a claim, because we are inherently lacking critical information.

- There are six context questions we must be able to answer:

  o Who is the speaker/author?

  o Who is the audience?

  o What is the content?

  o What is the delivery method?

  o What is the general context?

  o What is the intent?

CHAPTER 8

DECONTEXTUALIZATION

Now that we have seen the importance of getting the context right, and an easy way to make sure we're getting all the relevant parts of context, let's turn to decontextualization. Decontextualization is the act of omitting, obscuring, or removing the context pertinent to the discussion at hand. It is the opposite of contextualizing. Decontextualization is also a favorite tactic for presenting bad claims through twisted interpretations. This is an important issue, and a good example of how we can be misled into getting the context wrong – for any number of reasons.

Context manipulation changes everything. Whether we're leaving out any particular question from the list, or adding things like sarcastic tone, changes in context can change the entire meaning of the text or speech. In the Hitler example from the previous chapter, failing to note that the issue was about the benefits of highway systems, means that the entire conversation can be cast as some sort of Nazi-supporting rant. Similarly, failing to note the context of my own usage of that line, means that I could technically be cited as having claimed that, "Hitler was right." Yet, as bad as either case would be, media manipulation of context can be a lot worse, and can turn people into saints, monsters, or terrorists with ease.

For example, the Orlando Nightclub shooter (2016) was reported to have pledged allegiance to ISIS, while on the phone with authorities, during the massacre. With that "context," his actions seem to be a terrorist attack by the group against targets in the U.S. – a rather scary prospect. What was not reported – at least not in the same bombastic style, is that the shooter also pledged allegiance[32] to Al Qaeda and Hezbollah.

The thing to note here, by way of meaningful context, is that Al Qaeda and ISIS are not merely opposed to one another – they're actively trying to exterminate one another. In fact, as noted by William McCants' *The ISIS Apocalypse*, the pro-Al Qaeda groups worked with the U.S. military in 2006-2007 to kill off ISIS 1.0 in Iraq.[33] That bears repeating: Al Qaeda called up the U.S. forces in Iraq, and made a deal to kill off ISIS - because ISIS was too psycho even by Al Qaeda standards. Even more confusing was the supposed allegiance to Hezbollah, given that they are a Shi'a group – and ISIS considers all Shi'a to be their mortal enemies, killing them whenever they get a chance. Al Qaeda and Hezbollah are not on much better terms, either. There is scarcely a decent analogy of such inter-group hatred that can explain how ludicrous such claims of allegiance to these different groups are. Claiming allegiance to the Black Panthers, while also claiming allegiance to the KKK is in the right neighborhood, but not nearly violent enough to capture the difference.

In other words, the Orlando Nightclub shooter is unlikely to have been a member of any of those groups. Sure, he claimed to be a member, but I can claim to be the Pope – it does not make it so. Failing to note the different "allegiances," means that the Orlando Nightclub shooter was painted as some kind of a radicalized terrorist (lone wolf and other analogies abounding), instead of the lunatic with a questionable relation to reality that he was. This does not detract from the tragedy of the events, but it does demonstrate how missing a small piece of the context can shift the entire picture of reality.

Failing to understand the context is equivalent to looking at a single strand of a tapestry, and making judgments about the whole – or looking at a single pixel, and making judgments about the whole image. Even if we subscribe to the idea that the whole is only the sum of its parts, the lack of context means

---

32   Al Jazeera. *Orlando: Omar Mateen 'pledged loyalty to ISIL, others.'* https://www.aljazeera.com/news/2016/6/14/orlando-omar-mateen-pledged-loyalty-to-isil-others

33   McCants, William. *The ISIS Apocalypse*. New York: St. Martin's Press, 2015. Pg. 35.

that we're not even looking at all its parts (like the single line of decontextualized pixels in Chapter 7). The sheer silliness of the approach is apparent as soon as we attempt to apply it in circumstances where we do know the context. This very sentence is just a series of letters and spaces; but if we judge the entire thing by the 5th character (the space after the first word), we would have to assume that there is no sentence at all.

The real trick is recognizing that we are lacking context. Once this is known, the process of finding the context is easy, because we have a "known-unknown" – i.e. a thing we don't know, but are aware of our ignorance. The problem comes when we are faced with "unknown-unknowns," and are unaware that we're lacking information. The six questions in the previous chapter, and those in the next chapter, are useful precisely in helping us identify whether we're lacking context, and whether we need to go looking for additional answers before passing judgment.

While it is obvious that context is needed in order to make information functional, and make valid decisions, what is commonly forgotten is that it is <u>our responsibility</u> to find the context. Despite the push for Facebook and other media outlets to police content and remove fake news, the responsibility of fact-checking and contextualization falls to each individual alike. The shifting of blame for the lack of our own efforts may help us feel better, but it does nothing to fix the problems we create through our own ignorant actions. Thus, we must consider ourselves individually responsible for seeking and contextualizing information. Anything else is an abdication of our basic human feature - rationality.

Proper context was the key to something we mentioned in the previous chapter called "charitable reading." **Charitable reading** is simply the idea that, if we see or hear something that seems wrong, or out of place, we don't simply jump on it - like internet Trolls. Instead, we try and see if we can figure out what went wrong, and simply fix it – or in some cases alert the speaker/author as to the mistake, so they can fix it.

Here's an example: a friend is telling you about having watched the Hobbit, but he keeps referring to the main character as *Frodo*, when you know it should be *Bilbo*. Here, charitable reading would tell us that the speaker is merely mixing up the names, and we can either correct them, or we can ignore the mistake – substituting *Bilbo* for *Frodo* on our own.

Uncharitable reading, on the other hand, results in trolling. We can respond to catching the mistake by calling the person ignorant, by arguing that they have not actually seen the movie, that they are lying to us, etc. To be sure, it could be the case that our friend is, in fact, lying to us. However, most times, there are no nefarious designs behind such a mistake.

When we consider the context in which the mistake is made, we consider the speaker (a friend who does not generally lie to us), and we consider the intent (communicating some aspect of the story to us for entertainment purposes), it seems silly to assume the nefarious intent – and thus we read charitably almost by default. If we had a different context – say a dictator known for violence against his own people and for pushing ridiculous propaganda, then when another outlandish claim is made, even charitable reading seems to indicate that the claims are made with the purpose of sowing disinformation – hence, we should not trust them. With that in mind, we can look at different issues of decontextualization.

To begin with, decontextualization happens very often. We have decontextualized reporting by official media outlets – as in the noted case of the Orlando Nightclub shooter. We also have decontextualized reporting on a great deal of social media – with misleading headlines, and articles apparently crafted on the basis of reading only other people's headlines, instead of doing research. Then, we have the majority of comments – be it YouTube, or elsewhere – where the arguments made have little to no relation to the context, content, or intent of the author. We also, rather unfortunately, have science and science reporting turning to decontextualization for its own benefit. As Ben Goldacre notes (here[34] and elsewhere), this is becoming a common trope – where the results of a study are blown out of proportion, or are misconstrued.

With the background of decontextualization in mind, let's take a look at two specific examples of decontextualization, and the kinds of problems they create.

"Religion Causes Wars"

This claim is a good example of the idea that, when something is repeated enough, it becomes "true" - in the sense that it becomes believed by the general public. When this claim is made, the speaker will often back the claim with reference to the Crusades, and other such events. But once we dig into the

---

34   TED. *Ben Goldacre: Battling Bad Science.* https://youtu.be/h4MhbkWJzKk

claim, and look past the cosmetic veneer, once we actually look at things like the context of war, the whole thing collapses in a hurry. Let's consider a brief list of some major civilizations, and see if the claim holds up:

- The Greeks all shared a religion, and were engaged in constant war against each other. The wars were for political gain. Even when they fought the Persians – who were radically religiously different, they thought that it was political power (right to rule) they fought for, not religion.

- Alexander the Great also conquered a major chunk of the known world; these were not religious conquests, but political ones.

- The Romans were a religious people, and waged constant war against all their neighbors. Yet, the cause of wars was political power, and they generally allowed the conquered populace to worship their own gods. Internal struggles in Rome were not characterized by religious differences, but political maneuvering.

- The classical Chinese period was marked with a general unity of religious ideology, but also with incessant warfare (some wars lasting a whooping 550 years). The religious cause never became part of the justification for war, despite the wars lasting for centuries.

- The Indian subcontinent also generally shared religious thought, but the political wars of domination were frequent and bloody. A great example of the idea that "religion does **not** cause wars" can be found in the Bhagavad Gita – a Hindu religious text – that deals almost exclusively with an epic battle, and where one side literally has god as an advisor. Yet, the cause of war is not posited as religious difference, but the notion of "right" and "wrong" in terms of the right of the people to be ruled by a just ruler (defined in terms of ruling to protect the people vs. ruling for self-aggrandizement).

- The Mongols had a religion wildly different than the people they conquered. However, they did not conquer from religious justification – only from a political one. In fact, the Mongols perceived any attempts to convert to their religion as strange – because their religion was a religion for Mongols – much like religions limited to tribal membership. Genghis Khan also famously held a number of interfaith dialogues, allowed people to worship whatever they chose, and was instrumental in creating the office of the Dalai Lama (Buddhism).

- Both World Wars were, rather obviously, fought for political gain, not for religious reasons. The major players were all Christians, and not even the schism differences (Catholic-Protestant-East Orthodox) held any meaning for who joined which side. Rather famously, the Ottoman Empire (considered the last Islamic Caliphate) was a close ally of the German (Protestant) state in WWI – for clear political and economic reasons.

- The Jains are a pretty "hardcore" religious group, but have never been involved in violence of any kind – because absolute non-violence is the basis of Jainism.

- Chimpanzees have been observed, rather frequently, to engage in wars. However, they have not been observed to have religion. Chimp wars are all about territory and resources, never about beliefs.

Clearly, the similarity, difference, or presence of religion does not play a deciding role in whether wars happen. However, if we take certain wars out of context, or if we take certain populist appeals made in war as being the *only* justification for that war – taking away the context of economic, political, and social issues – we can certainly misconstrue wars as having a religious cause. For example, Communists were called "Godless heathens" during the Cold War but no one would argue that the source of the enmity was religious.

For speakers and authors with an anti-religious agenda, or those with a bias against particular religious groups, this kind of decontextualization allows them to make arguments based on the ignorance of their audience. It may be tempting, for example, to see the conflict between the Irish and British as a purely religious one – given the Catholic-Protestant difference. However, to reduce the conflict to a mere religious difference is to ignore the long history of brutal oppression of the Irish by the British; the political domination of an independent people by a more powerful force; and the prolonged public and political degradation and exploitation of the Irish. Once that context is introduced, the mere religious difference becomes rather silly.

"Al Ghazali's theological ideas are the reason why Baghdad (and Muslims in general) produced no scientific advancement after 1100"

This argument (paraphrased), made by Neil deGrasse Tyson,[35] is an example of atrocious failure to consider any form of context on two separate fronts. Worse, it came from a public figure held in high esteem by the general public, making the proliferation of this claim by average people all the more likely. The general idea behind Tyson's claim is that religion stifles science (known as the "conflict thesis," arising in the mid-1800's, which has been debunked by every field of science), and that Al Ghazali serves as a prime example of the claim. However, once we start to unpack the claim Tyson makes, the degree of misrepresentation becomes staggering. Let's look at the context of Al Ghazali, of the general historic state at the time, and of the timeframe Tyson uses.

- Al Ghazali (d. 1111), perhaps one of the most prolific and respected figures of the Islamic world (hundreds of texts authored by the age of 53), was a polymath and a prodigy. His style is characterized by deep research and understanding of any subject before commenting – a fact he stresses is necessary for any kind of meaningful academic work.

  I knew for sure that one cannot recognize what is unsound in any of the sciences unless he has such a grasp of the farthest reaches of that science that he is the equal of the most learned of those versed in the principles of that science...[36]

- Al Ghazali did have a disdain for scientism, as well as ignorant and limited approaches to studies – not for science in general. Thus, he argues that incomplete or decontextualized knowledge that attempts to encroach on unrelated spheres of study is a great evil.[37] For reference, what he means by this "encroachment" is something like taking theology and attempting to use it to make arguments in biology; in the process, one defiles both spheres of knowledge, and makes their own area of expertise look ignorant, by failing to realize its limits.[38] Clearly, the picture painted by Tyson

---

35   *The Golden Age of Islam Explained By Neil deGrasse Tyson.* https://www.youtube.com/watch?v=tJJLvoDg2_E

36   Al Ghazali. *Deliverance from Error.* Pg. 27.

37   *Ibid.* Pg. 32.

38   *Ibid.* Pg. 33.

does not quite fit the reality.

- Additionally, no scholar of Islam has ever come to the conclusion that "There's not a coherence to the practice of Islam until he [Al Ghazali] comes around." In fact, it would be quite a shock to every scholar of Islam and the Middle East in general, not to mention the people and rulers living there at the time, to learn that Islam was just a "pick your own ideas" system for nearly 500 years.

- In terms of the idea that Al Ghazali argued that "Manipulation of numbers is the work of the devil," a cursory analysis of his autobiography tells us that he believed and argued for something rather different:

  > *The mathematical sciences deal with arithmetic, geometry, and astronomy. But nothing in them entails denial or affirmation of religious matters. On the contrary, they concern **rigorously demonstrated facts which can in no wise be denied once they are known and understood**.*[39]

- As for the idea that the will of God governs the universe, Al Ghazali is neither the first nor the last theologian to take that position.[40] Yet, the idea that God has control over his own creation does not imply that the same creation is not orderly or that it is not comprehensible to the human mind, or worthy of study.

- The general context of Baghdad, prior to the 1100s, was as a world center of education and science. Ever since the 750s, the Abbasid state had invested significantly in science and philosophy – constructing what should have been one of the wonders of the world with the *House of Wisdom*.[41] All manner of science and research was encouraged, translations of foreign texts were paid for by their weight in gold, and a golden age of science, art, and philosophy took place. This was made possible by the security of the state, where all military and other threats were generally distant, and the military budget could be low – allowing the science and research budget to grow. Even with the Turkic invasion in 950, the political upheaval was relatively minor, and had no real impact on

---

39   *Ibid*. Pg. 31.

40   See: the *Mu'tazila* and *Ashari'* theological ideas which predate Al Ghazali.

41   *The House of Wisdom: Baghdad's Intellectual Powerhouse*. https://www.1001inventions.com/feature/house-of-wisdom/

the role and funding of research.

- Looking at the specific time period, 1100, we begin to see that Tyson fails to do any level of contextual research – despite there being some obvious historical problems with his claims. In 1098, the Islamic world suffered the first major military defeat, as the first Crusade burned and pillaged its way down the eastern coast of the Mediterranean. Jerusalem, one of the three sacred cities of Islam was destroyed – its population put to the sword. This new enemy was not merely highly destructive, it was now on the doorstep of the rest of the Islamic political world. With the safety of the empire now in question, the state shifted funding away from sciences, and towards the military (naturally). The timing of this shift in state budget happens to coincide with Tyson's date of choice.

- But it gets better. Tyson also fails to account for the fact that, for the next 89 years, the entire region would be engaged in a bloody war of local political domination, and expulsion of the Crusaders. With the liberation of Jerusalem in 1187, one might expect that a shift in funding might return science to its former prominence. However, that would ignore the fact that additional crusades were again launched against the region, and that, in 1258, the Mongols (coming in from the East) overran Baghdad – and wiped out the entire *House of Wisdom*, despoiling the city, and killing a large percentage of the population (genocide). Having wiped out the research center, and murdered the locals - including many scientists - is it any wonder that further scientific research did not come out of Baghdad? Does it seem at all coherent to assume that it was theology – not war and wholesale destruction of the region – that caused this calamity?

- Finally, Tyson does not account for the fact that, despite the loss of research in Baghdad, the rest of the Islamic world continued to produce major scientific and philosophical achievements.[42] Muslim India continued its investment in science and research, as did Egypt, Muslim Spain, etc. and frequently enough by the same scholars who fled the Crusaders or the Mongol invasions. In all these places, the writings of Al Ghazali were known, and he was highly respected. Yet, once the element of war, destruction, and genocidal levels of population loss are taken out of the equation, it seems that the Muslim world remained dedicated to science and research.

---

42   Britannica. *Mathematics in the Islamic World (8th-15th century)*. https://www.britannica.com/science/mathematics/Mathematics-in-the-Islamic-world-8th-15th-century

To simply discard the entirety of the political, historical, and personal context, is academically unforgivable. The fact that he brushes aside the Mongol invasion, as if the destruction of the greatest center of science in the world and the genocide of the locals plays no part in the presence of further research in the region, is inexcusable. Tyson is enough of an academic that he should have known that context matters. He should have known that not knowing the context disqualified him from speaking about the topic. And if he was too busy to do the research himself, he should have had the forethought to have an assistant do the work. As we see, the introduction of proper context into Tyson's claims takes the argument apart at the seams. It also discredits him as a speaker on any subject other than his actual area of expertise.

From the preceding, it should be clear how decontextualization can paint a highly-distorted picture of reality. The act of decontextualization may be a simple matter of ignorance, or it may be a malicious attempt to intentionally manipulate the audience into believing and acting on biased information, for the benefit of the speaker/author. In either case, it is <u>our responsibility</u> to make sure we understand and incorporate the context of the idea, event, or action into our understanding of it. The failure to do so, as demonstrated above, leads us to a rather false view of reality. As a result, the basis on which rests our judgements and decisions becomes unstable and divorced from reality – and thus we make incoherent decisions, with generally counterproductive results.

We've already seen the importance of context, but it is critical to drive the point home here. Decontextualization ultimately happens for one of three reasons (more on that in a second), but in all cases it actively damages the audience's ability to see the whole picture. By taking away context, intentionally or otherwise, we can end up with a radically different picture. Here are a few rather poignant examples of how removing context damages our ability to get anything like an accurate picture of who or what an individual was all about. Keep in mind, nothing in these descriptions is inaccurate.

- Turtle-killer, punches bricks (Super Mario)
- Unlicensed, Middle-eastern doctor (Jesus)
- Moustache aficionado (Stalin)
- Decorated war veteran with likely PTSD fails to get into art school (Hitler)

- Jungle-gym operator in central Asia threatens nuclear superpower (Osama bin Laden)

Decontextualization happens at all levels of society. People use it in arguments, politicians use it in debates, quack doctors use it to sell their "expertise," and too many scientists and academics use it to "prove" their theories. Decontextualization happens for one of three reasons:

1. **Ignorance**: when the speaker is unaware that there is context (unknown-unknowns)

2. **Relevance**: when the speaker knows that there is context they don't know about, does not know what it is exactly, but assumes it is irrelevant. (known-unknowns)

3. **Malice**: when the speaker knows the context, but withholds it for personal gain (known-knowns)

Ultimately, the malice option is intentional, premeditated lying. Lying happens when you want people to believe something – to get them to behave a certain way – which is of some benefit to you. But, you also know that the truth will not get them to behave that way, so you invent a fiction which, in your estimation, is sufficient to motivate the behavior you want.

As we will see, determining which kind of decontextualization may be in play will play an important role in our own analysis and evaluation.

SUMMARY

- Decontextualization is the act of removing context or context manipulation
  - Decontextualization attempts to distort the picture of reality by removing parts, or by making parts seem more or less important than they really are.
  - This is done in order to try to manipulate the audience into believing some claim, which the audience would not believe if they had the complete picture.
- Charitable reading is the act of treating the claims of other people as if:
  - The other person has valuable information
  - The other person is attempting to share the valuable information with you
  - Therefore, the audience should try to interpret what is said in a way that will make the claim as strong as possible (instead of nitpicking)
- Charitable reading makes sure that we are not decontextualizing the claims of others
- Uncharitable reading is trolling:
  - The assumption that the other person is trying to deceive us
  - Therefore, the audience should reject all claims, on any possible grounds
- Uncharitable reading is inherently about decontextualization
- Decontextualization can only happen by:
  - Ignorance of the speaker
  - Choice about relevance of information made by the speaker
  - Malicious misrepresentation (lying) by the speaker.

CHAPTER 9

CONTEXT TOOLBOX

In considering the six questions of context in Chapter 7, we left the least developed question 5 (General Context) for later analysis because it dealt with a number of secondary questions. Here, we want to delve into some of those questions, specifically how to formulate them and what we can get out of them. These can be used on written texts as well as in discussion settings, where the questions we have can be addressed by a speaker directly. These kinds of questions are intended to be understood as part of a toolbox of understanding and communication.

A crucial part of the process of gathering context is a proper engagement with the claim. We commonly take an aggressive, combative, argumentative tone when we engage with claims. This is a problem, whether we're dealing with a text or with people. In a way, it is a sign of reacting, rather than responding. When using critical thinking on others, you have to start with the assumption that the person is not trying to lie or trick you. This is charitable reading. In fact, assume that they know something you don't, and try to understand that lesson. Don't try to argue; try to understand. People can hear the difference in your tone, and if you're just trying to understand, then they're willing to work with you (more often, anyway). But if you're argumentative, then they get defensive, and nothing good happens.

If you think you've found a contradiction in their thinking, don't start off with *"this is why you're wrong!"* Instead, ask them a series of easy questions, like *"hey, does X work like this?"* When you get them to agree or disagree, then you have a base from which to ask the difficult questions. These are questions like, *"if X does this, and Y does that, how do they work together?"* And if they contradict one of their earlier answers, then you follow up with a, *"how does that get around the Z you said earlier?"*

Notice that, if you don't get argumentative and hostile, *you are not trying to prove them wrong.* Instead, you are working with them to figure out whether their idea works or not. If they do have a good way to explain their idea, then maybe they're right and you're wrong. But if they don't have a good way to explain their idea, they'll see it too – and that's how people change their minds. Remember that reactiveness is what happens when the person gets overly emotional – and feeling attacked and getting defensive are emotional states. So, avoid causing those emotional states in yourself or others, and reason can work just fine. With texts, we have to play the role of the speaker. That means that we have to be very charitable, in order to make sure we don't misrepresent the claim.

We have three sets of questions to ask. The first set of questions are about clarification. With those questions, we are looking to make sure that we fully understand the claim. The second set of questions are about the implications of the claim through conditional questions. Finally, the third set of questions are about proof and evidence. In all three cases, we should **assume that the claim works**, and act as if we are trying our best to present it to the best of our ability. That way, we read charitably and we can get the best perspective on both the questions and answers.

Questions of Clarification

For clarification questions, we need to understand what is being said. In this way, we do our best to make sure that we are not misunderstanding the claim, that we are not reading uncharitably, that we are not decontextualizing, and that we are not becoming Trolls or *Fake News*.

1. <u>**What do you mean by that?**</u>

We are often faced with statements that elicit a strong reaction – positive or negative. However, often enough the reaction actually comes from phrasing or word choice – not the meaning or content. This question should be the most common part of your toolbox for understanding context. It tries to look behind the façade of words and phrases to get at the heart of content.

When we think we understand the claim, we should offer a summary and give the speaker a chance to correct our understanding (if the speaker is available). If there is no speaker available, we should write out our summary of the claim, and see if it lines up with the text and if it really covers the whole point the text was aiming to make.

2. <u>**Can you say that in a different way?**</u>

Piggybacking off the previous question, and for the same reasons, asking for a clarification in different terms is a very useful tool for making sure the terms used are what we assume them to mean. This question is particularly good at getting past jargon and other technical language, and simplifying the statement or idea.

If we're doing this part on our own, keep in mind the following: you can't meaningfully rephrase a claim if you don't have a decent understanding of the claim. You can think of this in terms of foreign languages. You can easily memorize a song in a language you don't speak (you memorize the sounds in order). But, you still have no idea what's actually being said. That means that you can't explain to anyone what those sounds you made mean - even though you know how to make the sounds.[43]

3. <u>**Can you give an example?**</u>

Examples are a great way to imagine the concept in practice. It both helps us as the audience to wrap our heads around the idea, and it also helps the speaker by making them put the idea into practical terms. This kind of direct "application" also allows us to better imagine some consequences and other issues that are at the core of some later questions.

If you can't give an example, it's because you don't have a good grasp on the idea. If we can give

---

43   How many people can sing along to *Despacito*, and how many of those people actually understand the words they are singing?

examples about fictional characters (like Superman v Batman), then we can certainly give examples about any other issue we understand.

4. <u>Why do you think that?</u>

Where the first three questions focused on clarifying the idea itself, this one is about clarifying the speaker's justification for their belief. Instead of asking for the description of the claim, we're asking about its justification. By doing so, we can examine the system that's supposed to be holding up the idea. You can think of this in terms of physical buildings: some foundations are solid, others are less so. Poor foundations make for shaky buildings, and it is often more profitable to go after the foundations of a claim than the claim itself. This is true whether the claim is going to be torn down or repaired.

When we look for the justification of a claim, we often find that at least part of that justification comes from a different source – an argument or study the speaker has read elsewhere. When that is the case, we have to go and locate that source, and check the validity of that claim as well. Why?

We noted some of these issues in Chapter 5. When we rely on information or arguments from others, we introduce an additional risk of things going wrong. If the claim or study being cited is somehow faulty, or is not functional, then it can't be used to meaningfully support the claim in question. If the speaker/author misunderstood the claim they are using, or if they picked a claim that is not functional in their own argument, then it does not provide the kind of support they are hoping for. Finally, it happens that some speakers are willing to intentionally make up a source and the claim in order to back up their own argument. This is why it is important to actually do our work and check where the original ideas are coming from, in order to make sure they actually hold up the claim in the way we think they do.

5. <u>Are absolute terms used?</u>

Absolute terms (never, always, must, can't, etc.) make the claims absolute – also known as categorical claims. While they can make the arguments appear to be stronger, they are also supremely dangerous. Against an absolute claim, we only need one counter-example to make the whole thing collapse. As a general rule, outside of mathematics, we want to stay away from absolute claims. Even the universal speed limit of light can apparently be broken by *Quantum Entanglement*. So, to claim that it is impossible to go faster than the speed of light (a categorical claim) would be false.

A lot of categorical claims can be softened, by couching them in relative terms. For example, "<u>We do not believe</u> that it is possible to break the speed of light, <u>under general conditions</u>." The underlined sections couch the claim in a way that lets us treat the speed of light as a functional absolute, while not setting up the claim for total collapse if the other side brings up quantum entanglement or in case some new discovery proves us wrong.

Conditional Questions

Conditional questions are "if-then" questions, which explore the implications of an idea. With implications, we ask questions to check what the idea would mean, *if it were true*. This lets us get a grip on how ideas work together, understand implications and limits, and whether you're looking at a rule or an exception. Again, you should assume that the idea/claim is true.

Rules and Exceptions

When we look at a claim, it is very important to understand whether it is presented as a rule or as an exception. Rules are the kinds of statements that generally apply to everything. Exceptions are the kinds of statements that are not covered under rules, because there is some kind of a contextual oddity that makes the rule not work. As a rule, it is illegal to go over the speed limit. As an exception, it is perfectly legal to do so. As we start to analyze the meaning of the claim, and go looking for counterexamples, we need to know if we're looking for counterexamples to rules, or to the much more limited exceptions. If the claim/idea does not say which it is, then go with whatever makes more sense. Rules are about "general" statements that hold true most of the time. Exceptions are much more rare, and happen under specific, limited circumstances.

When we do things like make laws, we make general laws for the majority of cases. We make exceptions for exceptional circumstances that somehow change the context of the situation so much that the general rule would not fulfil the purpose of the law. What we don't do (or should not do) is make general laws based on rare exceptions, instead of the most common context. We have a law that killing other people is prohibited (because that's the most common context), and then we add an exception for self-defense (because that comes up less often). You don't want to make killing people legal in general, just because sometimes it may be necessary for self-defense.

The final thing to note about absolute language is that it is sometimes well hidden. We don't have to use words like "always, never, etc." to have an absolute claim. In the decontextualization chapter, we used the example of the phrase, "**Religion causes wars.**" This 3-word claim has two absolute terms hiding in it.

The first one is "religion." Because it is unlimited by other ideas, the term actually means "all religion, ever, everywhere." So, if I were to invent a religion right now, it too would cause wars. Also, because it is unlimited, all we have to do is point to Jainism – an eastern religion which prohibits any form of violence or harm at all, for any reason, and we have a counterexample that breaks the whole claim.

The second absolute term is "causes." The word "to cause" has a number of different meanings, depending on the context. However, in this phrase, it is used to indicate that there is a *causal relation* between the first term (religion) and the third term (war). So, if you have religion, then you have a causal relation – kind of a chain - that inevitably leads to war. In terms of logic, if we say that A causes B, then all we need to know is whether A is true. If it is, then B **must** be true. Let's use a simple example:

If A, then B.

If your car is running, then it has gas.

Is there any scenario where your (gas-powered) car could be running without gas? No. As soon as you know that the car is running, you know that it **must** have gas. That first part is impossible unless the second part is also true. Apply that to "Religion causes wars" and you have something like, *If there is a religion, then wars must be caused by it.* Again, a single example of any religion that has not supported a war, even one I make up right now, is enough to show that the claim is broken, because it is absolute.

Now, you might look at this analysis and complain that this is misrepresenting the claim. "Obviously," that's not what the speaker meant to say, and so on. However, unless there is some kind of an explanation the speaker gives where they explain their idea in more detail, or that can be gained by reasonably charitable reading, all the reader has to go on (at the beginning) is exactly what the speaker said. We can, and should, check whether the claim is intended as an absolute or not by looking at the language in the rest of the claim (as we did in the slavery example).

Implications:

What are implications? Implications are conclusions we can draw from given information, which are not explicitly stated in that information. In essence, they're additional conclusions we can extract on the basis of the stated information.

A lot of our communication happens by implication, instead of direct statements. Let's say you have a travel mug full of liquid filth (diarrhea) – for some reason. Your friend comes in, winded, out of breath, and reaches for the travel mug with the clear intention to drink the contents. What would you say in that moment? Probably something like *"That's diarrhea!"*
Your friend hears you, and proceeds to drink it anyway. Then with a look of shock and disgust, they turn to you and ask, *"Why didn't you tell me not to drink it?!"*

And here, your friend is right - technically. You did not actually tell them **not to drink it**. You told them what the contents of the travel mug were. The **implication** is that diarrhea is not something we want to drink. And so, merely telling someone what it is, should imply that they should not drink it.

Implications will tell us what else is true, what else is not true, and so on – allowing us to fill in a lot more of the picture. Implications are important, because they allow us to pull additional information and context from the original claim. They tell us about how the claim is supposed to work.

If you've ever watched any of the police procedural shows, like *Law and Order*, or if you're familiar with *Sherlock Holmes*, you have seen implications at work – implications are really the stars of these kinds of shows. Implications are how we work our way up to meaningful conclusions from limited information. In fact, if you play games like *Sudoku*, you use implications to solve the puzzles, because you are working with a lot of "if this is a 3, then the other 3's in this section must be in **these** columns, and they cannot be in **those** rows, etc."

Limits:

What are limits? Limits are the elements that constrain the claim/idea in an important way. They generally tell us how far the claim actually extends, or – if you prefer – the functional parameters of the claim. This is another way we can tell the difference between rules and exceptions. If we think about the exception for legally driving above the speed limit, the exception is **limited** by the kinds of contextual features that must be true, to in order to give us the exception to the rule and make speeding legal. That's why the off-duty police officer going home is not allowed to drive over the speed limit – because the contextual features that otherwise allow him to break the general rule (officer on duty, traveling to location of a call) are no longer present.

Some things are true all the time, while other things are only true in specific circumstances. Limits tell us about how far the truth of a claim actually goes. For example, $2+2 = 4$ is true all the time. On the other hand, $a^2+b^2 = c^2$ is true only if we are dealing with triangles which have a right angle. Those conditions (triangle, right triangle) are the limits of how far the Pythagorean Theorem actually goes. If you have a problem that can't be turned into a right triangle, then the Pythagorean theorem is not functional for us in that context.

When we run into a claim that does not seem to work, a charitable approach is to try to imagine it not as a rule, but as an exception. That way, the claim might still work. But, to turn a claim into an exceptional claim, we have to imagine what kinds of limits must be in place for that claim to work. As we add these limits, the scope of the claim (what it actually affects) gets smaller and smaller. We want to do this, because we are not interested in breaking a claim, we're interested in making it work. So, if we can make it work – even if it's only under very narrow conditions – we still have something that's true. It may not be very useful, but we did the best we could with what we were given.

Onto the questions themselves:

1. <u>**Can you think of a case where the statement is not true?**</u>

This question is primarily directed at you, as the audience. If you can think of a case where the claim is not true, then you have additional material to work with. The initial question, however, depends on the type of claim. If a claim is historical, then you probably cannot use a hypothetical counter-example (because the "what if's" of history are too vague to really make a claim). If the claim is abstract, then you can use both historical and hypothetical examples (because you can test a hypothetical idea against reality and against other imaginary ideas). If you can come up with a counter-example, then you have to look at the context of that example, to make sure it fits the context of the original idea. For example, if the initial claim is that "smart people do not make dumb mistakes," your counterexample has to make sure that the "smart person" is smart in the field where they made the mistake – otherwise, they're still a "dumb person," and the counter-example does not work.

We want to know if there is a counter example, because if there is one, then we start to develop some new limits for the claim, and can have a better idea of how it actually applies.

2. <u>**If the claim is true, what else must be true?**</u>

By asking this question, we're trying to draw out the implications of the original claim. Sometimes the claim is solid, but the "side-effects" still cause serious logical problems. An easy way to think of this is in terms of ideas that are good on paper, but that fail miserably in reality. The failure in reality does not come from the claim itself, but from the implications that are unresolved.

Additionally, some claims are hard to verify on their own. If you don't have a particle accelerator, it is very difficult to directly test a claim from CERN. But, claims have implications, and we can often check the implications of a claim a lot easier than the claim itself. By looking for the implications, we can often find issues that either break a claim or that impose new limits on it.

3. <u>**If the claim is true, what can't be true?**</u>

The flip side of the previous question, this question looks at the implications that are supposed to make certain ideas impossible – if the claim is true. For example, the idea that "electing a woman president means the society is not sexist," implies that any society where women were elected to the highest office can't be a sexist society. That is, if you find sexism in such a society (let's specify: sexism against women) then the claim is false. We can then look at Pakistan, India, Indonesia, etc. and see that the claim is false (all have had female Prime Ministers, but all have major sexism issues).

Questions 2 and 3 seem almost identical. However, I like to present them as separate questions, to get you to think about the different implications separately and focus on them specifically. Too often, when we combine these into a single step, we gloss over either positive or negative claims and do not pay nearly as much attention as we should.

Questions of Evidence:

The final set of questions deal with the evidence that is presented for a claim. Evidence is the justification which supports the claim.

1. <u>**What kind of evidence do we need?**</u>

Depending on the kind of idea/claim being presented, the kinds of evidence will differ. What is important is to first decide what kind of proof is necessary for the claim, and then take a look at what is available (next question). We often follow this process in reverse, and as a result, we are swayed by our biases to believe or disbelieve. If we want to believe X, then we'll find a way to make the lack of evidence somehow sufficient. If we don't want to believe X, then we'll always ask for more proof.[44] The trick to critical thinking is not just critically examining others; it is also critically examining ourselves. By first establishing the requirements of proof needed, we can curb our biases when we look at the actual proof offered.

It can be very helpful to write out the kinds of proof we would need. This has two benefits. First, it commits us to a standard of evidence, so we can't weasel our way out later. Second, it gives us a clear sense of whether our requirements are coherent.

I am sure you've encountered people who say something like, "*I will never change my mind about*

---

44   These kinds of mental gymnastics are commonly called *Moving the Goalposts* fallacy

X." Quite often, these kinds of claims can be about things like religion, or climate change, or something along those lines. Now, look at that statement again. It is irrational.

Let's say the person here believes X instead of Y. Why do they believe that? They have to have some kind of a way that they created that belief. There has to be some kind of a justification for that position. What the person is saying is that, if they had better evidence for believing Y instead of X, they would not believe Y - even if that evidence was, by their standards, the kind of evidence that they should otherwise believe. This is no different than a person sticking fingers in their ears and yelling "La-la-la!" in a discussion.

The one possible exception here comes from **axioms**. Since axioms are things you *assume* to be true, without proof, we might find people holding onto these kinds of ideas no matter what. However, even with axioms, the whole set of ideas still needs to be coherent (as per Chapter 6). That means that the implications of the axioms still have to end up lining up with the axioms themselves (this is a matter of internal coherence). If Bob axiomatically believes that all people are good and would never harm anyone, then he either has to account for genocidal maniacs and rapists in a way that does not contradict his axiom about goodness of people, or the axiom is broken. In essence, while you can believe in any axioms you like, they still have to come together in a coherent way. You can think of this as the functionality requirement for infinite interpretations.

2. <u>What kind of evidence is available?</u>

By looking at the available evidence, we can make critical judgments about claims. Working from the previous question, we can measure the available evidence against the necessary evidence, and draw a clear conclusion. We can also note what evidence is missing, and determine whether this kind of evidence might reasonably be found with some additional effort.

This is actually the process of developing new ideas. We come up with an idea, check its meaning and implications, and then check its evidence. If we're seeing strong indicators that evidence may be available, or that we might generate it by doing work ourselves (surveys, compiling data, etc.) that tells us that our project may be a good idea to pursue. If the indications are weak, or there are no ways of pursuing evidence, then we have good reason to think of the project as non-functional.

3. __Is this interpretation the most probable one?__

In philosophy, anything that you can actually imagine is possible. Impossible is only that which breaks one of the laws of logic – and since you cannot even actually imagine that, there's a relatively low chance of the argument being of that variety. So, it is logically possible that I can turn into a bat and fly away (there is nothing self-contradictory there). It may not be physically possible for me to do that, but that's a different matter. Notable exceptions include arguments that are self-contradictory (because they're poorly thought out), so what you're imagining is not what you think it is.[45]

However, the mere *possibility* of the explanation is not enough for functionality. Is it possible that aliens came 5,000 years ago and built all the things we recognize as being classically Egyptian? Yes, it is. That is to say, I can imagine that happening. Is that explanation the most **plausible** explanation of the development of classical Egyptian architecture? No. This is important: the mere possibility of an interpretation (which happens as soon as it does not directly contradict itself), is no proof that it is actually probable (most likely true interpretation).

When faced with a possible explanation, we must ask whether there are alternative explanations, which account for all the facts in the claim, that also provide a different conclusion. If there are, then we must ask whether any of the options requires us to perform seemingly unnecessary mental gymnastics to make the facts fit that conclusion. If one explanation requires all sorts of additional interpretive tricks (Aliens!), while the other one does not, the least complex one is the more likely plausible one.

4. __Can this make sense if I use a different interpretation?__

Sometimes, the problem is that we're trying to read things literally, when they're supposed to be understood metaphorically, or they are idioms, etc. If an idea does not work – or is implausible – try to change the way you're interpreting it and see if that makes more sense. The main limit for this question is whether that kind of interpretation works across the entire claim.

If I can make the claim work by reading it metaphorically, but I have to read the same ideas as being literal in my justification, then I have a contradiction. That is, if I have to perform mental gymnastics

---

45   The actually impossible generally comes down to breaking one of the Three Laws of Logic (https://digitalcommons. brockport.edu/cgi/viewcontent.cgi?article=1046&context=phil_exl)

to make the ideas work between justifications and conclusions, then I have a bad reading of the claim.

5. <u>Can the claim be salvaged?</u>

If the claim does not seem to work – if the justification is just not good enough – we can call it a day there. This is the academic approach: we are merely evaluating the functionality of the claim, as stated. This approach is fine for telling us whether this specific claim, exactly as stated, works. While this can be a good approach in an academic setting, because of how academia works, it's not really the best approach to the search for some version of truth – which ought to be our primary goal.

If our aim is the truth, or let's say the best approximation of truth that we can get to, then we are actually interested not just in what the claim actually says. Instead, we are interested in what we can get out of it. Every kernel of truth is precious and should be pulled from a claim. Even when a claim is terribly bad, we could still learn from it. At least, we can identify what went wrong, and be better equipped to identify other claims as being wrong along those same lines.

Therefore, if the claim seems not to work, we should ask ourselves whether we can salvage it. Can we build up a better justification for that conclusion? Perhaps we can interpret the data in a more functional way. Perhaps we have access to better information we can use. Perhaps we can't get a rule out of the claim, but we could at least come up with some kind of an exception – even if it is possible only under crazy circumstances (this is actually very important in studying ethics). You can think of this as the last attempt to read the claim as charitably as possible. Yes, we are the ones doing all the work, not the original author. But, we are ultimately doing it for our own benefit of getting something valuable for our time and effort dealing with the claim.

If we can make the claim work at all, then we can conclude that we have a functional claim. Perhaps the original claim was garbage, but we got a functional one out of the mess. But if we can't salvage it, then we are forced to conclude that the claim is garbage all the way through.

As you have no doubt noticed, some of these questions are for the author/speaker, others are for you as the audience. Critical thinking is a reciprocal activity: both sides need to participate. You can also use these questions as guidelines for building your own arguments. By anticipating these questions, you can speak or write in a way that helps address these questions before they're brought up. In writing, this also helps you clarify your thinking, by forcing you to answer these questions in a way that would be satisfactory to others. If you cannot answer them, your position is weak, and needs to either be fixed or abandoned.

For written texts, the process is a bit more difficult, because we have to read through very carefully, focus on word choice, focus on literary structure, etc. in order to draw out the answers. Sometimes, we get lucky, and can find an interview with the author, where some of these questions were asked. Most times, we have to engage in thorough reading and charitable reading, and even then, the results are not guaranteed.

SUMMARY

- To get the full context, we ask three sets of questions as part of the "general context" point.

- In all cases, we need to approach the claim charitably:

  ○ Assume the speaker has something valuable to offer through the claim

  ○ Assume claim is true for purposes of analysis

- Questions of Clarification are intended to ensure that we understand the claim clearly and entirely.

  ○ Unless you do understand a claim clearly and entirely, you can't agree or disagree with it - because you don't know what it is.

- Questions of Implications are intended to provide additional information about the claim - the kind of information that we might be more easily able to check on our own.

  ○ If the implications of the claim don't add up with reality, then the claim can't be true.

- Questions of Evidence are intended to provide us with a clear set of requirements for verifying a claim, testing the evidence, making sure our reading is appropriate, and checking if we can provide additional/better justification for the claim.

- Getting the answers to these questions, in this order, provides us with critical context to make our determination about the validity of the claim.

CHAPTER 10

ZHENGMING AND WU-WEI

When engaged in examining ideas and critical thinking, it is crucial to get our terms and ideas right. Context, as we already talked about, helps us do so in one way. But we also need to make sure that we understand the "thing" itself, so that we can make sure we're looking at the right context. Let's make that a bit clearer by example:

This is a dumbbell. We can look at the context of its weight, color, workout plans using these weights, marketing using this color, etc. to get the context. And, despite being right about several context issues, we can still be entirely wrong about the context of **this** dumbbell. How? Because its context here is… paperweight! Or it could be a doorstop. Or a murder weapon. Or any number of other uses I could put it to, that your initial context examination did not cover. So, what did we miss? Why were we wrong?

We were wrong, because we did not understand the thing itself. Sure, it is a dumbbell, and our assessment was partially right. But, we missed the fact that a name – in this case "dumbbell" – does not give us the whole story. What matters is not the name, but the meaning – and meaning depends on how it is used, not on sounds we make when we speak – or symbols we use when we write. A nice summary of this point can be found in the Islamic principle of law that says: *"regard is given to the meaning, not the name (term)."* What they meant is that the use of the term was irrelevant to law – what mattered is the meaning the term took on.

Classical Chinese philosophy found itself faced with a similar issue: how do we actually know what a thing is? Simply giving things names is not enough – as seen in our example. So, they came up with a pair of related concepts that would solve the problem: *zhengming* and *wu-wei*.

Zhengming translates into "rectification of names." To rectify means to put a thing straight, or right; to fix a thing – as in to place it so that it does not move. What the Chinese meant by *zhengming* is getting our definitions properly set, so that their meanings were clear. This required defining the thing in context – so that the relations of a thing were properly understood.[46] At the end of the process of defining the thing, they gave this list of attributes a name. Once we encounter a thing, we check its performance against our list of definitions and attributes – and when we find a set of performance attributes that fits, we have a name to put to it – and thus we know what a thing is.

For the Classical Chinese authors, as for us today, the simple use of a term could be misleading. Having a title assigned to a thing does not mean that it actually functions in a way we would expect. As a simple example, we have the old joke:

---

46   This idea of getting relations right is a major part of Confucianism, specifically the *5 Bonds* that define the 5 major social relations.

"What do you call a boomerang that does not come back when you throw it? A stick."

On a more serious note, we have corporate titles that imply certain abilities, skill sets, and performance, but often do not actually meet any of those expectations. A manager who does not manage, or who mismanages, cannot really be considered a manager – regardless of the title. A patriot who betrays his country is not a patriot, he is a traitor. The danger, of course, is that assuming performance on the basis of a title gets the whole thing backwards. One should earn the title by performance, not assume performance by title. Here, the famous example of the great Confucian scholar Mencius's conversation with King Xuan can help us clarify the issue:

- *King Xuan of Ch'i asked, 'Is it true that T'ang banished Chieh, and King Wu marched against Tchou?'*

- *'It is so recorded,' answered Mencius.*

- *'Is regicide permissible?'*

- *'He who mutilates benevolence is a mutilator; he who cripples rightness is a crippler; and a man who is both a mutilator and a crippler is an [outlaw]. I have heard of the punishment of the "[outlaw] Tchou", but I have not heard of any regicide.'*[47]

For Mencius, the execution of King Tchou (regicide) is justified. This is a prime example of *zhengming*; the *definition* of a king is what matters – not his title. By definition, not only is Tchou not actually a king, he is an outcast/outlaw. By the definition of an outlaw, the punishment and execution is justified, and even necessary. The fact that Tchou was called a "king" is irrelevant – anyone can call themselves whatever they want, it does not make it so.

So, now we have a term that helps us remember that identification should be a product of performance, not the other way around. However, we can still misidentify the expected performance, as with the dumbbell. Here, the second term comes into play.

Wu-wei translates into "action without action." While this may sound very "oriental" and "Zen," what the Chinese meant by this term was: *letting a thing reveal what it is, without our interference.* With the dumbbell, we made assumptions, we *projected* our ideas of definitions on the object. We forced our

---

47   Mencius. *Mencius.* Ed, Tr. D.C. Lau. New York: Penguin Books, 2004. Pg. 23.

preconceived notions onto it. This projection is what often gets us into trouble, because it relies on our assumptions and stereotypes, instead of an analysis. *Wu-wei,* on the other hand, cuts off our projections, and lets the thing show us what it is, by what it does and how it is used. This keeps us from assuming we already know the answer.

As a more practical example, stereotypes and other such heuristic shortcuts are a great tool for everyday use.[48] When you go shopping, you don't check whether your milk is made of milk, or whether your bananas are made of bananas. You stereotype the shape, weight, and other easily discernible features of an object, and get your groceries. This is fine for highly repetitive and mechanical tasks. How often do you really check whether the car on the road next to you is really a car (maybe it's really a Papier-mâché car)? Imagine if you stared intently at every car on the road, to check whether it is a car. That would be a very short trip, because you would quickly end up driving into something. Why? Because your focus was not where it should have been (the road). You can get by just fine stereotyping cars on the road, which keeps you from driving into walls.

Stereotyping is great, because it lets us make decisions quickly on the basis of previous knowledge. This way, you can move through your day without having to stop at every one of the tens of thousands of decisions you will have to make.

However, when dealing with a new idea, or with an idea that is suddenly in question – as is the case every time we face a claim that affects us – we can't afford to simply stereotype the claim. We need to actually stop, and turn our full attention to what's going on. Because this claim is now the focus of our attention, we no longer assume that our previous knowledge and experience is good enough. Instead, we have to make sure that we understand *this specific thing* in front of us. As we have seen, knowing about other dumbbells is of no help regarding what this particular dumbbell is.

When *zhengming* and *wu-wei* are coupled together, we have a list of definitions by which we will

---

48   The term stereotypes has a negative connotation, though in many ways undeservedly so. We all stereotype objects, places, people, and situations all day long. We have to, if we are going to get through the day. The real problem comes when we take a statistical generality (e.g. Target employees wear red), and try to apply it to individuals ("this person must work at Target, because they're wearing red"). Statistics work on very large sample sizes, but tell us nothing about **this** or **that individual**. That's why we can all understand what it means that the average American family has 2.4 children, but would be very surprised if someone thought that this statistic meant that Bob has 40% of little Timmy in a basement freezer.

judge the performance of things, and thus classify them accurately – while keeping our assumptions in check, so that we learn what a thing is, by observation. This kind of thinking is why we value "fresh eyes" on a project – preconceived notions can get us stuck in a rut, while approaching the problem without such assumptions can allow us to see the problem and possible solutions in an entirely different light.

An additional benefit of this kind of thinking is in keeping us from falsely assuming that we share definitions, just because we share a term. Reverend Gary Hall's response[49] to Richard Dawkins is a great example of recognizing this false assumption. Given Dawkins's position on God (Dawkins is a hardcore atheist), Rev. Hall replied, *"I don't believe in the God you don't believe in either."*

Theology aside, Rev. Hall's statement cuts to the heart of the issue: while both men use the same term ("God"), their respective definitions of God are so radically different that any debate on the topic is actually impossible – they can't help but talk right past each other (also known as *incommensurability*). However, despite these radical differences, we often engage in all sorts of debates and discussions, failing to realize that we're never actually speaking about the same topic – all because the terminology *sounds* the same.

Think of it this way: the Greeks called Zeus a "God" and Hindus call Brahman "God." The term is the same when translated into English. However, the definitions of Zeus and Brahman are so different that Hindus don't believe in Zeus and Greeks don't believe in Brahman – even though both sides would say that they believe in God. Suddenly, simply talking about what "God" is and is not becomes an issue, because until we define what we mean by the term, we have no meaningful way of determining what we are actually speaking about. That means that we have no way of meaningfully agreeing or disagreeing. The same issue is present in the Dawkins/Rev. Hall example. Because their definitions of the term "God" are so different, Rev. Hall gets to actually agree with Dawkins, because he also does not believe in Dawkins's definition of God – any more than he believes in the Zeus definition of God.

With *zhengming* and *wu-wei* as our guiding principles, we should be on constant lookout for definitions and the way in which they're being used. It is crucial to realize that this process is not about being

---

49   The Washington Post. *From Comedy to National Cathedral.* https://www.washingtonpost.com/lifestyle/style/from-comedy-to-national-cathedral/2013/08/01/683906e2-f884-11e2-8e84-c56731a202fb_story.html?utm_term=.b5a133739fd4

right or wrong; it is about being coherent. Whether we subscribe to Dawkins's definition of God, Rev. Hall's definition of God, or neither, is irrelevant. What matters is whether the terms we use match in their meaning, and thus allow us to speak about the same topic. Without a shared understanding of ideas, we cannot actually communicate (even if sometimes it may sound as if we can).

The obvious points where *zhengming* and *wu-wei* are applied is for terms that have known plurality of meanings (like the definition of "God" across different religions). But those are not the only cases. In fact, when we engage with claims, one of the big questions is how to understand the statements we encounter. There are a lot of ways that ideas can be understood, and depending on the kind of understanding we apply, we can end up with different meanings of the same phrase.

Just because people are using words does not mean that we know what those words are supposed to mean. There is more than one way of understanding both the words that are being used and ideas that are being presented. You have to know which kind of interpretation works and is intended for what idea. Which option is being used usually depends on context. Here are some options:

1. **Literal** – the statement should be understood as is, no interpretation necessary beyond a dictionary definition

   a. Statements like *Today is Tuesday*.

2. **Metaphorical** – the words imply something other than the literal meaning

   a. "Cheating is wrong" actually means "don't cheat" and "cheaters are morally bad people" by implication of the term *wrong*

3. **Idiomatic** – weird phrases specific to a language, etc.

   a. "He is so hot" means that someone is attractive – unless you're talking about a person who has a fever.

4. **Extended** – extends meaning, by analogy, to other issues

   a. If murder is wrong, then intentionally aiding someone in committing murder is also wrong – because the action leads to murder – even if you don't pull the trigger yourself.

5. **Sarcasm/joke** – saying one thing but meaning its opposite.

   a. "Yeah, right" can mean agreement, or – if you say it with the right inflection – it means a hard "no."

6. **Plural** – more than one meaning at a time.

   a. Let's say that teaching is prohibited while drunk. Why? Because inebriation means that you don't know what you're saying. Well, the same can be applied if you are legally high on painkillers (say, post-surgery), or if you are extremely tired, emotionally unstable, etc. Even though only one thing is said, the full plurality of the meanings is implied, because of the goal of the initial statement.

As a result, when we are working to decipher the meanings of terms, to understand some idea, we have to be careful about not only the definitions, but also the specific ways in which these words are being used in their context. Unfortunately, the dictionary definition of "Yeah" and "right" do not tell us about the context which may be sarcastic, and then we draw the very wrong conclusion about what is being said.

Now that we have the core factors of critical thinking in hand, we turn towards the *Claim Shredder Method*. As a methodology, the *Claim Shredder Method* is intended to give you a clear, concise, and shared methodology for applying critical thinking to the claims of your choice. The key feature to remember is that this method is universally valid. That is, you can use it for cybersecurity threat analysis, you can use it for biology, you can use it for art history, you can use it to fix your relationship, etc. The method is simply the way to rationally engage with any claim, in any field, in order to understand it, to understand what it means, and to determine whether it is valid.

SUMMARY

- In any claim or discussion, we must clearly define what terms mean (*zhegming*).

- If we don't have well-defined terms, then the meaning of our words is never clear to anyone, not even ourselves.

- In order to check whether a thing or a term fits a definition, we have to observe what it does on its own – without interruption (*wu-wei*).

  - A definition by itself is great, but we need to make sure that the thing or term actually fits that definition, or a different one. Remember the paperweight-dumbbell.

- Heuristics like stereotyping are great ways to make speedy decisions when you already know how things work. But, you can't use them when you're dealing with a new situation or when you're facing a new claim, because, in these cases **you don't know** how things work.

- Using a similar/same term but with different definitions means that we are not communicating with each other, even though it may sound like we're talking about the same thing (incommensurability).

- For claims, knowing which kind of interpretation is being used is important.

  - "Yeah, right" can mean "*I agree*," or "*I definitely don't agree*" – depending on the kind of interpretation used.

CHAPTER 11

THE SYSTEM

At this point, we have covered all the major points we need to cover in order to seriously engage in critical thinking. All that's left now is to put it all together into a streamlined process we can use. A key point is that the process needs to be a clear, straightforward, transparent, step-by-step method of going from the claim to the conclusion about its validity. That way, anyone can look at the work, understand what is happening, determine whether any mistakes have been made, and pick up the process at any point and complete it.

We understand the problem before us – namely the issue that claims cannot be accepted at face value, and so have to be checked by us, before they can be accepted. The process of checking is best accomplished by the use of context, in order to examine, clarify, and justify the claim. The resulting idea is then checked for functionality and against evidence, to arrive at the conclusion on whether it should be taken seriously or not. Throughout this process, context reigns supreme.

However, and this is the other running theme, we can't get to context in any way other than reason.

On the path to context by reason, we are constantly stymied by emotional extremes that threaten to derail our efforts – the emotional extremes of others, and our own. The problem is made continually worse by the varieties of media (including social media and marketing) whose headlines encourage outrage and emotional instability, for click-bait purposes. As a result, we must remain vigilant to avoid falling into this trap, and to keep our wits about us – that we may meaningfully use reason.

The system we are about to explore is a rather straightforward one – and only has two phases: 1) Argument Buildup and 2) Decision. In Argument Buildup, we are clarifying the context of the claim; we try to build up the argument that the claim is making, which means that we need to understand what is and is not being said, how, where, why, etc. This way, when we engage with the claim, we are sure that we did not misunderstand or misrepresent the claim. In the Decision step, we are clarifying the justification, we make a decision about the validity and value of the argument we created, by looking back at the kinds of information we got during the first step.

This flowchart is the final product, and we will be returning to it for the rest of the book.

The CLAIM SHREDDER CLAIM Method

PHASE 1 - ARGUMENT BUILDUP

PHASE 2 - DECISION

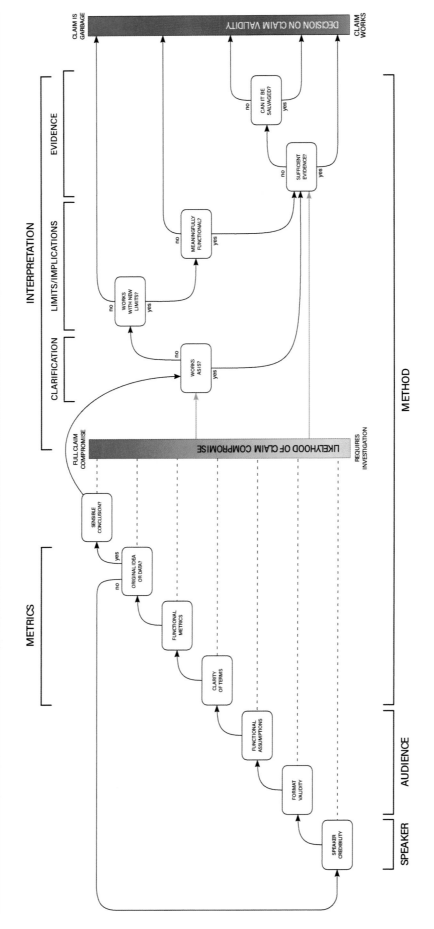

METHOD

All data is biased, there are infinite possible interpretations.
▲ Focus on FUNCTIONALITY

METRICS

- What is being measured?
- How is it being measured?
- Are terms and definitions clear?

BEWARE: statistics games

INTERPRETATION

- Clarify the claim
- Check implications and limits
- Evaluate the evidence
- Is a more functional interpretation available?
- If broken, can the claim be salvaged?

AUDIENCE

- Who is the intended recipient?
- Explain nuance in phrasing
- Clarify speaker intent
- Formatting and data type?
- Implicit assumptions?

SPEAKER

- Speaker qualifications?
- Speaker affiliations?
- Speaker history?
- Is this a sales pitch?
- Speaker intent?

During the two phases, we ask four questions:

1. Who is the speaker?

2. Who is the intended audience?

3. What is the methodology (metrics)?

4. What is the methodology (interpretation)?

You may be wondering: *what happened to the rest of our context questions?* As you will see, all the questions have been compressed into these four.

So, now you may be wondering: *why did we bother with the long-form questions?*

By first giving you the full scope of the questions, where they're heading, why we ask them, etc. you should have developed a strong sense of why context matters, and the different ways it can get manipulated. You should also have a full understanding of the kinds of processes that lie behind the questions we are asking, and the kinds of ideas we are trying to uncover – and for what purpose. In essence, the long-form approach is about making sure that you can derive these ideas on your own, even if you forget the exact phrasing we use here.

The system we are about to engage in is a kind of short-cut for the long process we have already explored. It works like a formula in mathematics; knowing the formula alone is not enough, we have to know the theory behind it and how to derive it on our own, so that we can make full use of it.

You may also be wondering what happened to that initial conversation about emotion and reason. The rational approach that keeps emotions in check is a prerequisite to critical thinking, playing a key foundational role in being able to ask questions and properly understand answers. If we are reacting instead of responding, no amount of clarification, context, or explanation will be helpful. As a result, you need to start by shifting away from emotional reactions, embracing the rational approach, and then engaging with the claim. In essence, take a deep breath to clear your head, and then start in on the claim.

There are three starting ideas we want to keep in mind here. First, the entirety of the *Claim Shredder Method* is based on asking questions – just as discussed in Chapters 7 and 9. In fact, you will see most of those questions repeated, though we will focus on a slightly different and expanded set of reasons to use them. Read the questions again, read the explanations again: knowing which questions to ask, how, and why is a critical feature of the critical thinking process. Going over the questions again will help you remember them. Taking notes is even better.

Additionally, as noted in Chapter 9, sometimes we are lucky and the speaker is right there and we can ask them questions directly. That makes our jobs easier through direct interaction with the speaker. Other times, we don't have the speaker, so we have to take on the role of the speaker. That is, we have to answer the questions for them. To do that, we have to look into who the author is/was, when they wrote, what their big ideas were, and other questions that give us a sense of the kinds of ideas the author might have had. That way, when we answer questions for them, we are as accurate as we can be in our answers. As always, charitable reading is absolutely critical for this process. If you act like a troll, you will misrepresent the idea, and that means that you will not evaluate it properly.

The second point is that when we ask questions, we must do so sincerely. What does that mean? It means that you don't decide in advance whether the claim that you are evaluating is right or wrong. Instead, you genuinely take the idea as something worth exploring, and then ask questions so that you can understand it better. No matter what you think about the claim at the start, you must be willing to be wrong. If you happen to be wrong, then you have learned something new. If you happen to be right, then you have learned how people have this wrong idea and why it is wrong.

Alternately, since most people generally don't even like to think that they could be wrong, we can think of this approach as sincerely trying to figure out why someone would come to the conclusion that the claim is making. It does not matter what the claim is, you are exploring how the speaker got there, and why.

But why should we do this? People have a pretty good sense when someone is being dismissive, rude, argumentative, etc. And when people sense that, they get emotional, defensive, reactive, and the whole ability to use reason is gone. That means that neither person is getting anywhere. But we also have a pretty good sense when someone is genuinely engaging with us. And that's when people get talkative, they start thinking, and they actually start examining ideas.

In my own classes, if a student tells me that they believe in something outrageous, I never shut them down. Instead, I ask them to repeat it slowly, while I write it out on the board. Then I ask a whole lot of questions, meaningfully – because I legitimately want to know what it is exactly that they think, and why they think that. It turns out that it's really hard to have a bad idea for a good reason. Bad ideas are usually supported by very shaky justifications (which is what makes them bad) – if there is even a justification there. By asking a bunch of questions, the student actually thinks their way through the idea. If the idea is bad, the student realizes that the idea they pitched is not working. We then try to salvage it – rephrase it, alter the language to make it work, go from a rule to an exception, etc. At this point, I am *arguing for their side* as best I can (and encourage other students to do so as well). But if that does not work, and we are all clearly trying to make it work, the student is usually ready to accept the outcome and give up on the idea, because they saw that it does not work – not even when a whole lot of people were trying their best to make it work.

Now, if I had just shut them down with a "no," or something similar, they would have gotten defensive (emotional), and they would have stopped thinking. And then, they would hold on to the bad idea. By sincerely engaging, we are collaborating on exploring a claim. If there is nothing there, we both see it plain as day. This makes it easier for people to accept the outcome, and to actually change their minds, instead of building up a grudge. Throughout the process all we're really doing is being charitable, instead of being trolls.

Finally, and I think this is crucial for understanding what it means to have a conversation, debate, and so on: **you cannot change anyone's mind for them, on any issue, ever**. All you can do is understand them, and then try to ask meaningful questions. Even if their idea is wrong, you can't do anything about it. The only way someone changes their mind is if they change it themselves. This is the same process as religious conversion (to, or away from, any faith or agnosticism/atheism). No one else can convert you, you have to convert yourself. With that in mind, it's a lot easier to stop trying to "win" and try to meaningfully engage with people. You are discussing things with them for your benefit – not for theirs. That means that you should be the one learning – regardless of whether they're right or wrong. If they also learn something, good for them, but that's not why we do this.

If we're engaged in an actual conversation, we don't need to worry about convincing anyone of anything. We are engaged in a free exchange of ideas. I can explain my position to you - if you care to hear it - and you can explain yours to me. Maybe I like your position better and end up agreeing with you - or maybe you agree with my position. Maybe we find a middle ground, or maybe we stay at our respective positions. Either way, we can both learn something and understand each other better. Maybe we discover that we're both actually wrong. What is not going to happen is that I will somehow say some magic words, and suddenly you will agree with me. All I can do is explain myself, and give you something to potentially think about. Everything after that is up to you.

The Research

As we try to answer the questions in the *Claim Shredder*, we are going to have to do some research. That may sound a bit scary to some of you, but fear not – research is not that hard. There are a few key ideas you need to understand, and the rest is just practice. Let's start with what we mean by that term.

When we say research, in our context, what we mean is something like: google it, read, check for basic consistency (that there are no contradictions), look up terminology, translate some jargon, etc. In essence, we're trying to make sure we understand what's going on, before we engage with the claim itself. None of this is particularly difficult, although it does tend to take time.

The big thing to note here is that the kind of research needed for all the questions we will be asking is just public information. There is no magical research tool that you need to know how to use. There is nothing that you need to download, no subscription fees, etc. It is all the kind of information that you can pull up through Google and other such sites. Occasionally, you may need to use something like JSTOR - a paid service for peer-reviewed journals. If you are a student at a college, you have access to that for free. If you are not a student, you can still go through your local library, or use Google Scholar to see if there is a version that is freely accessible online.

So, what should you be using for research?

Oxford English Dictionary (https://www.oed.com/) is a must for any kind of research. Making sure that you clearly understand the language used is step one in understanding what is being said. It's occasionally very good to check your word choices, even when you think you're sure you understand the language. I do so quite frequently as well. An easy way to Google terms in the OED is to type in the word into the search bar, and add "oed" after it. The first result is the OED result. In case you need more linguistic detail, you can also use the Online Etymology Dictionary (https://www.etymonline.com) to find the correct kind of connotation and nuance in specific expressions.

If the claim you're looking at uses a lot of jargon, you want to google "define [word or phrase you're looking for]" and the name of the field in which you're looking. For example, the word "sprite" can have a number of very different meanings. But if you google "define sprite programming" the results are very different than if you just searched for "define sprite."

There are also sites dedicated to translating jargon, by field. For technology jargon, I would recommend TechTerms (https://techterms.com/). As you do this kind of research, you will undoubtedly find additional sites that you can rely on for the kind of research you're looking for, and then you can focus on those results first.

As much as I may not like it, you can use Wikipedia for certain kinds of general information research. I would advise not relying on it fully – since it's not a very reliable source in many fields (which you notice when you're an expert in a field, and then you look at pages about that field). However, it works well enough to get a general idea and to give you some starting points for looking for specific terms, connections, etc. You really want to look at the sources (footnotes at the bottom of the article), because that can give you something more tangible to read.

LinkedIn is a decent source for contemporary speakers/authors – especially for journalists and such. It will give you a basic overview of their education, employment, etc. Similarly, people's personal and professional pages (like a University page about a tenured professor) will usually have good information as well.

If you happen to be taking a philosophy class, the Stanford Encyclopedia of Philosophy (https://plato.stanford.edu/) can be a good resource, as can the Internet Encyclopedia of Philosophy (https://iep.utm.edu/). Be warned, however, these can be fairly jargon-filled and dense.

Finally, since most of us have computers in our pockets (smartphones), we should learn to use them for research. If your phone's voice commands are activated, you can just yell at your phone to give you a definition of a term, without needing to put down the book, open your computer, etc. As soon as you are not absolutely sure that you could define the term for someone else, you should be looking it up. Worst case, you already knew the definition. Best case, you can correct a misunderstanding early on, so that you're not an hour into your analysis when you realize that a crucial idea means something entirely different. Also, if you're seeing an author use a term in a funny way (often seen when someone uses a verb as a noun or noun as a verb, or when a normal word is suddenly *italicized*), make sure you search for the definition of the term and add their name to the search. That way, if they have some funny twist on the meaning of the word, you can catch that early on.

As you get into the habit of looking things up, your work will get better in several ways:

- You will get faster at looking up the exact kinds of things you need and sorting through the results to find what you're looking for. This is just practice.

- You will need to look up fewer things, because your knowledge on the subject will increase (this is a long-term benefit, since you will already know something about other claims on that topic).

- Your analyses will be significantly better when you can back up every step with a source.

- Your own writing will benefit from the same ability to do research quickly and efficiently. This helps across all your academic work, and also helps in most jobs – since eventually most of you will have to write up a report or an analysis of one kind or another.

With all that in mind, let's take a look at the *Claim Shredder Method*.

CHAPTER 12

WHO IS THE SPEAKER?

The first question is: who is the speaker? This can also mean who is the author, who is the source, etc. Who is it that is making the claim? We care about the speaker, because the credibility and expertise of the speaker play a part in how we understand the claim they make. As an example, we'll take the phrase:

"Iran is not engaged in nuclear weapons proliferation"

How would you rate the credibility of this claim when it's made by Bob the hobo? What about if it is made by Iran, or by Russia? What about if it is made by Mossad (the Israeli intelligence Agency – like the CIA)?

Bob the hobo, being a hobo, is understood to be a less than reliable source of truth on the nuclear weapons programs of foreign governments. So, you can dismiss him as a meaningful source of information. If Iran makes that claim, we understand that they have an incentive in not being perceived as trying to make nukes, so their statement is taken with a whole bag of salt. If Russia makes the claim, it is better. However, Russia is a resource ally of Iran, so we have to take their claims with a grain of salt. But if Mossad makes that claim, most everybody will believe it. Why? Because of who the speaker is: Mossad sees Iran as an existential threat to themselves and their state, and they are very good at their job (intelligence gathering). So, if Mossad makes that claim, we believe them far more easily and without the need for additional proof.

There are five questions we ask about the speaker. These are:

1. Is he/she an expert?

    a. Is he/she an expert in that specific field?

    b. How do you know?

    c. What are his/her qualifications?

        i. Lack of qualifications is not a disqualifying factor, but qualification is an issue that can come up, and so it is something we want to keep in mind and account for.

2. Who is their employer (including self-employment)?

    a. What are their relevant interests?

    b. What are their Biases?

    c. What is their Agenda?

    d. What is their profit source?

3. What is their history?

    a. What is their history of making such claims?

    b. What is their history of being right about such claims?

4. Is this a sales pitch?

5. What is the speaker's intent?

The first question – **are they an expert?** – is focused on the idea that expertise has to be verified. That means that everyone has a right to their opinion, but not all opinions are equal. Let's say that Bob comes on a news show and is introduced as having worked for the Democratic Party (or Republican Party) for 20 years. That's great. What did he do there? Just having worked for them does not mean anything useful. Bob could have been a janitor for 20 years, or he could have been in charge of handling sensitive information, or writing party platforms. You have no idea, because "working for the party for 20 years" is insufficient. That's why we ask so many questions there. We ask for qualifications and proof, as a way of confirming the expertise.

A point to keep in mind is that the speaker's lack of expertise does not mean that they are, by default, wrong (e.g. a 14 year old Ukrainian hacker can discover a serious exploit). Instead, it is a thing we have to note and account for. Different fields have different levels of access by non-experts. You can teach yourself how to be a hacker. You can't run your own particle accelerator tests, because you can't build your own particle accelerator. But, you can teach yourself physics and then rationally analyze the results obtained by people with access to the accelerator.

The second question – **who is their employer (including self-employment)?** – is there because we know that different organizations may interpret or even twist ideas to suit their purposes. If an organization depends on there being a lot of crime (say, they're selling home protection systems), they're not very likely to come out and say that crime is at an all-time low, and getting better. Why not? Because that's the end of their job. That may be a cynical perspective, but it is fairly realistic. If the employer is shady, or if the claim is closely related to their biases/agenda/interests, we need to keep an eye on the issue and account for it later.

An important point here is that **everybody has an agenda.** That is, everyone who is publicly making a claim is only doing so because they have a reason for doing it. It may be for publication, for prestige, for exposure, for fun, for the benefit of mankind, etc. Every speaker has an agenda, because if they did not have a reason to speak, they would not speak. That does not mean that everyone is just out for themselves. Instead, it means that just because you see that this person got a benefit of some kind out of their claim, it does not mean that you should disregard them - but you should pay attention. Again, we note if there is a possible conflicting motive, and we will have to account for it later.

The third question – **what is their history?** – is pretty crucial. When we take all the click-bait into account, it's easy to see why making crazy claims is to the benefit of the speaker. But, the thing with crazy claims is that – being crazy – they fall pretty flat on their face. This is a "boy who cried wolf" kind of issue. If you see that the speaker keeps making these kinds of claims, but is rarely right (or is never right), then this looks like another cry for attention. Again, don't dismiss the claim, but it's a thing to account for.

The fourth question - **is this a sales pitch?** – is one we often forget to ask, to our detriment. We know that a sales pitch is designed to get us to buy a thing that we may not need – or even want. It is designed to make us believe that, by buying some object/service X, our lives will be magically made better, or easier, safer, etc. That's why the sales pitch consists of first building up a problem and then delivering the magical solution. So, when we hear a sales pitch, we need to be cautious about accepting the kinds of "threats" or "problems" being made i.e. the "reasons" why we should want or concern ourselves with something.

The final question – **what is the speaker's intent?** – is always a difficult question. As noted in Chapter 7, we cannot see intent directly. Therefore, we have to infer intent based on a variety of contextual features. It's easy to jump to emotional conclusions about intent and to ascribe all sorts of positive or negative intentions to a speaker. It is far more difficult to reserve judgment until all the information is collected and the situation can be fully assessed.

As a result, while we are asking the question about intent here, we are not fully answering it. We are only starting to collect the information we will need, and will return to this issue again and again. At this point, we are primarily interested in getting information about possible intentions by understanding the speaker, looking at their expertise, background, employer, etc. If we can see a clear agenda running through their work, that gives us an indication for a possible direction of their intention and is an issue we will have to account for.

So, how does one go about "accounting" for something?

We'll get into this more in the second phase, but for now, let's summarize it like this: as we attempt to clarify the justification of a claim, we will have to look for evidence that supports the claim. The kind of evidence we need depends on how strong the claim is and how compromised it might be. When concerning ourselves about the validity of the claim – like, when we're looking at a sales pitch – we also need the kind of evidence that will assure us that we're not being misled. In essence, every time we have to "account for an issue," we will need more proof, more evidence that the claim is legit – because we have less and less to lean on for support.

Let's say we have a speaker who is a confirmed expert who works for a company that just does straight analysis of certain kinds of events. They have a history of getting it right, and they have a history of not siding with anyone out of bias or interest. On those three points, we don't need any additional evidence, because there are no issues to worry about. Now, let's say that the speaker is also recommending a product, and has a disclaimer that he's paid by the company that makes the product. Now we have to worry about the claim being a sales pitch. So, our evidence will have to overcome that worry.

These questions, as you may have noted, are just an expanded version of our first context question about the speaker from Chapter 7. By using follow-up questions to ask about details, we are just ensuring that we have enough context to fully answer this question. As you will see in our case study, even such introductory questions can reveal quite a bit about what is going on with the claim - even before we've actually turned to examine the claim.

CASE STUDY

WHO IS THE SPEAKER?

To illustrate the way the *Claim Shredder Method* actually works, we will take a look at a real-life example. We will use this specific case study for the rest of the book, stopping at the end of each section of the *Claim Shredder* to apply the lessons of that section to get a clear and direct sense of how that process plays out.

The case study is the October 4, 2018 story called *The Big Hack: How China Used a Tiny Chip to Infiltrate U.S. Companies*. The story appeared on Bloomberg Businessweek. If you'd like to take a look at the story yourself, and follow along with the process, you can access the original story.[50] For those of you who prefer to just read the case study, here's the TL;DR version of the story:

Supermicro is the largest manufacturer of motherboards in the world and is a U.S. company. But, like many other U.S. companies, their product is actually manufactured in China. Their motherboards are used by essentially everyone: from Apple and Amazon, to the CIA. However, the Chinese government forced the Chinese factories to insert a tiny chip into those motherboards. That additional chip then allowed the Chinese government to effectively see everything that happens on every computer using those motherboards (including the ones with impeccable security). In short, we all got hacked.

When this story broke, the entire cybersecurity world was in chaos. People were literally running around server stacks, pulling out units, and looking for the offending chip with a

---

50   Bloomberg Businessweek. *The Big Hack: How China Used a Tiny Chip to Infiltrate U.S. Companies.* https://www.bloomberg.com/news/features/2018-10-04/the-big-hack-how-china-used-a-tiny-chip-to-infiltrate-america-s-top-companies

magnifying glass. NPR ran a week of non-stop coverage, filled with experts who did not wonder *whether* we're all screwed, but only *how* screwed we are - very screwed, by the way, according to the experts.

The story had massive impact, lots of coverage, it affected the stock market, forced government agencies to comment, etc. Thus, it is a great example to check with *The Claim Shredder*. As an additional feature, this part of the case study will feature screenshots and other visuals of what the results of various searches revealed. This should allow you to follow along more easily.

1.   Is the speaker an expert?

Looking at the article, we see the "byline" right under the title and graphic. That tells us who the speaker is

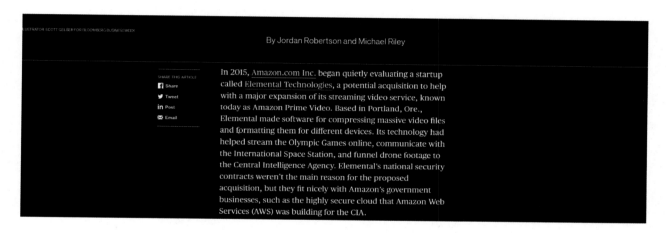

The authors of the article are Jordan Robertson and Michael Riley. If you have never heard of them, don't worry, neither did I when I sat down to go through the story. So, what do we do? Google their names plus the name of the publication (Bloomberg Businessweek). Let's start with the first person - Jordan Robertson - because the order of the byline usually indicates who is the primary author. When we do this, we should get hits - we can see their profiles on Bloomberg and on Linkedin, and on Twitter, etc.

Now, where to start? Linkedin usually has education, prior employment, job titles, etc. so, that's the first place I looked.

Education

University of California, Berkeley
Master of Journalism degree, Documentary Filmmaking and Business Reporting
2006

San Jose State University
SJSU
Bachelor of Science degree, Journalism
2001

It appears that we have a journalist, who is a non-expert in cybersecurity. But, maybe his earlier jobs might have equipped him with the kinds of expertise we want to look for. Scroll down, and we get this:

Experience

B
Cybersecurity Reporter
Bloomberg News
2011 – Present · 7 yrs
Washington D.C. Metro Area

AP
Technology Reporter
The Associated Press
2005 – 2011 · 6 yrs
San Francisco Bay Area

We have a tech-reporting job at the Associated Press, but that's not really the right kind of credentials, because its focus is not cybersecurity. The Bloomberg position is in cybersecurity, which is better. However, and we'll see this in a moment, Bloomberg is not an expert publication in the cybersecurity field. So, the articles are written for a non-expert audience. It's still possible (if unlikely) that Jordan Robertson is an expert, so we'll note it here.

Then I hit this interview (below) that Jordan Robertson gave. Notice that he's not talking about his skill, but about his need for expert sources. That means that he is still a non-expert, but writes about cybersecurity by getting experts to talk to him. This is not all that surprising for journalists in highly complex and technical fields, but again, it is a thing to note.

> Security is an area that's so fast moving. It's also very source dependent. That's a benefit of DC; there are lots of security people passing through all the time.
>
> It's different than covering a company. It's no less intense on source building. Security is so broad; you don't know where next great tip will come from. You could get a call from an independent person you've never heard of or talked to and they can call with great tip.
>
> It's also important to meet with a lot of people and get your name out there. Great tips come from everywhere. It's source development. Reading Twitter and other sites are good for ideas, but sources are critical. People are finding cool stuff all the time and you want to be the one they call.

My Conclusion: Speaker is not an expert.

2.   Who is their employer?

Now that I knew a bit about our author, it was time to take a look at the employer, the interests, agendas, etc. To prepare for this, I skimmed several other articles by the author - to make sure that this was not somehow an unusual article for him. This matters because you want to see if there is a pattern of the kinds of articles the employer is publishing. If the article is a standard kind of article the author writes, then you have a good sense of what's going on with the employer. If the article is radically different, then it is possible that something was overlooked and the outcome was not business as usual for the employer. That is, we want to make sure we're not misrepresenting the employer based on one incident.

A pattern emerged from this author. Because of the pattern, I knew that this is business as usual at Bloomberg Businessweek

■ Updated on September 29, 2017, 1:33 PM EDT

The Equifax Hack Has the Hallmarks of State-Sponsored Pros

The handoff to more sophisticated hackers is among the evidence that led some investigators inside Equifax to suspect a nation-state was behind the hack. Many of the tools used were Chinese, and these people say the Equifax breach has the hallmarks of similar intrusions in recent years at giant health insurer Anthem Inc. and the U.S. Office of Personnel Management; both were ultimately attributed to hackers working for Chinese intelligence.

Others involved in the investigation aren't so sure, saying the evidence is inconclusive at best or points in other directions. One person briefed on the probe being conducted

There are several click-bait headlines for articles authored by Jordan Robertson. Here, "click-bait" means that the headline and the content of the article don't match. The headline reads with certainty that it was "state-sponsored pros" that hacked Equifax (i.e. our usual suspects: Russia, China, or North Korea). The content of the article, on the other hand, is much less certain - "inconclusive at best or points in other directions."

Bloomberg is not a tabloid. Therefore, the question for me became: *why would a respectable journalist at a respectable institution produce click-bait headlines?* And there was more than one such headline. The most common answer is that they have an incentive to do so. So, I ran a search on "Bloomberg News" and "incentives," and got the answer:

Bloomberg News Pays Reporters More If Their Stories Move Markets

Julia La Roche Dec. 11, 2013, 3:01 PM

This practice is not widespread in the financial news industry, and journalists we spoke to from other outlets were not aware that it is used at Bloomberg. We also canvassed traders, bankers and public relations professionals. None of them had heard this before, either.

Most of the people we spoke to, especially traders, were startled to hear about this practice, worrying that it might create an incentive for Bloomberg reporters to "push" or stretch stories with the specific aim of moving markets. Traders react instantly to headlines and news stories, and the decisions they make often make or lose significant amounts of money.

We asked Bloomberg about the practice. A company spokesperson acknowledged it.

In short, if a story (headlines are the gateway to the story) gets a market reaction, the author of the story gets paid more. Now the click-bait headlines make sense. In fact, there is an incentive for breaking the story first, getting clicks, getting reactions from traders, etc. So, I asked myself, how much of a market reaction did *The Big Hack* story get?

Supermicro lost 47% of their stock value in 48 hours! Actually, they lost 60.5% of stock value on day one - October 4 (stock fell from $21.35 to $8.45), but it bounced back to around $11 at market close. That's a major move. You can bet that this level of reaction means a bonus for Jordan Robertson. But, we can't assume the story is false just because the results line up with the employer's agenda. Any other major cybersecurity story would likely get the markets to move as well. The bonus pay is just that, a bonus. Again, we will have to account for this issue later on.

My Conclusion: The employer has an agenda to affect the markets, and is willing to incentivize behavior to get it done.

3.   What is their History?

Having already skimmed a number of articles by the author, I had seen another pattern emerge:

> company's challenges may go still deeper. <u>One U.S. government official said</u> leads being pursued by investigators include the possibility that the hackers had help from someone inside the company. "We have no evidence of

> <u>Two people who worked with Mauldin</u> at Equifax say she seemed to be putting the right programs in place, or trying to.

> However, there are signs that Smith and others were aware something far more serious was going on. The investigation in March was described internally as "a top-secret project" and one that Smith was overseeing personally, <u>according to one person with direct knowledge of the matter.</u>

Equifax Inc. learned about a major breach of its computer systems in March -- almost five months before the date it has publicly disclosed, <u>according to three people familiar with the situation.</u>

What we're seeing here is that Jordan Robertson seems to offer little or no real attribution to his sources (telling his readers who his sources actually are - in terms of names, positions, etc.). Look at the underlined content there. Recall the issue of "Bob, who has worked for the Democratic Party for 20 years" we brought up earlier. When we can't see who the source is, we have to rely on the speaker here to vet the sources appropriately. This is a problem for the author, because he is not an expert.

If he were an expert, then we might be able to rely on his expertise to parse through the information on our behalf. If he were to share his sources, then we could check their expertise and decide whether they are trustworthy or not for ourselves. But here, the speaker is a non-expert who can't parse through the information on his own, and we don't know who the sources are - so we can't try to check their expertise on our own.

If we rely on a non-expert to decide which sources are functional, and we can't know who those sources are, we can end up with all sorts of problematic claims. For example, "Trump was the greatest president in U.S. history" - according to one set of anonymous sources - but he is "the literal incarnation of Satan," according to a different set of anonymous sources. Unless we get some kind of additional information, we have nothing to really go on.

Of course, many journalists use anonymous sources. Sometimes, naming the source will expose them, get them fired, jailed, etc. Journalists have a right to protect their confidential sources. However, in those cases, we usually have something tangible that the source gives us. They either pass on information or other things that can be verified by the journalist. For example, Edward Snowden handed over a lot of data and files to Glenn Greenwald (a journalist) to verify the claims he was making. That's why, even if Snowden had remained anonymous, we could trust the anonymous source - because we would be trusting the information that we could verify. At the very least, expert journalists act as a vetting process (the official term is "gatekeepers"), because their own expertise tells them whether the story from the source actually works or not. But a non-expert journalist and anonymous sources means that we're likely to be left in the dark.

At this point, we have a lot of information on the first author. Running a similar search on Michael Riley - the second author - reveals more of the same.

The Denver Post
8 yrs

Washington Correspondent
Jan 2009 – Oct 2010 · 1 yr 10 mos
Washington D.C. Metro Area

Directed the Post's coverage from Washington.

National Reporter
2002 – Dec 2008 · 6 yrs
Greater Denver Area

Covered Hurricane Katrina, Pope John Paul II in Mexico, a school shooting in Erfurt, Germany, the breakdown of justice on American Indian reservations, Mormon gangs in Utah, and the 2008 Democratic National Convention.

Bloomberg
8 yrs 1 mo

Investigative Reporter
Jan 2017 – Present · 1 yr 10 mos
Washington D.C. Metro Area

I write on cyber security, technology and national security for Bloomberg's Projects & Investigations team

Cyber Security Reporter
Oct 2010 – Dec 2016 · 6 yrs 3 mos

Cyber security reporter for Bloomberg News and Bloomberg Businessweek

Education

University of Minnesota-Twin Cities
Master's degree, Political Science and Government

Williams College
Bachelor's Degree, Philosophy

Michael Riley @MichaelRileyDC · 29 Sep 2017
Chinese hacking tools and a possible insider. Behind the scenes of the Equifax breach w/ @jordanr1000 @anita_sharpe

We have a non-expert, a journalist, working for Bloomberg, using clickbait headlines, etc. He has 7 cybersecurity stories - 5 of those are with Jordan Robertson - and 4 of those 5 are on *The Big Hack*.

My Conclusion: Checkered history, at best.

4.   Is this a sales pitch?

Since the author is not suggesting that we buy anything, hire anyone, etc. the story is not a sales pitch. On the other hand, the author is telling us that Supermicro is compromised, and that (predictably) led a lot of people to sell the stock - so that might be a version of a sales pitch.

My Conclusion: there is no direct sales pitch.

5.   What is the speaker's intent?

This one is a bit tough at this stage. We have a non-expert author, working for a company that incentivizes breaking news, whose use of anonymous sources - along with lack of expertise - creates an unverifiable foundation for justification, and which seems to feed into creating misleading click-bait headlines. All this seems to be fine with his employer (Bloomberg) who keeps on publishing the stories. What makes the intent hard to actually gauge here is that sometimes journalists get lucky, catch a major story, and we don't want to dismiss the whole thing as another click-bait story without doing all of our due diligence. That said, if I had to take a stab at the motive, I would assume the incentive-model at Bloomberg has a lot to do with this story, at least the style in which it is presented, and the kind of over-the-top claims that pop up. In short, it all reads as if the truth of the story may not be as relevant to the author as the idea of getting that story published.

Of course, since this is the first step of the process, we're not looking to draw the final conclusion. For me, I took screenshots and made notes on the side as I did the research - including the kinds of issues that came up that will need to be accounted for later.

As I was preparing this chapter for publication, one of my editors (Michael Owens) sent me a 2019 Washington Post link to, _Bloomberg reporter of the challenged "Big Hack" story gets promoted_.[51] It's worth a read, because it additionally indicates that the kind of issues we noted about Bloomberg (incentivizing the clicks), may be part of the way this publisher generally operates. To be sure, I did not have this information when I ran through the story the first time, and I don't want to introduce its findings here, because they happened long after the fact. But, I now have a piece of information about Bloomberg that I can rely on in all my future dealings with them and their journalists.

What about you? You should ask yourself a few questions at the end of every step, and note your own answers. While we are asking the following questions with the words like "feel," we're not relying on emotions here. These phrases are English idioms, which stand in for something like, _"given the information so far, and the idea that every point of weakness will require additional proof for the claim to be valid, which way do you believe the story is most likely to go - valid or garbage?"_ While these questions are specific to our case study, you can use a more general version of these questions for any claim.

- How do you feel about the source of the claim?
- Has the research given you a sense of trust, or a sense of unease?
- Why? (try to be as precise as possible)
- How do you feel about the information on Bloomberg News incentives?
- What kinds of evidence would you need to feel more secure about this source of information?

---

51   Washington Post. _Bloomberg reporter of the challenged "Bih Hack" story gets promoted._ https://www.washingtonpost.com/opinions/2019/09/17/bloomberg-reporter-challenged-big-hack-story-gets-promoted/

CHAPTER 13

WHO IS THE AUDIENCE?

The second context question we ask is: who is the audience? By that, we mean, who is the intended recipient of the communication? We care about the audience, because understanding that bit of context explains things like the nuance of phrasing, as well as speaker intentions.

When we communicate, we inherently take into account whom we are speaking to. This is why a doctor speaks one way to a child patient, a different way to an adult, and a completely different way to other doctors – because the same words can mean different things, and some words are and are not acceptable depending on that context. A doctor will note a "subdural hematoma" on the patient's chart, but might explain the same issue as a "boo-boo" to a 3-year old. That difference is there because the charts are intended for one audience, while the spoken explanation is intended for a different one.

Here, we ask two questions:

1. **What is the formatting and data type?**
   a. How is the data presented?

b. What kind of data is presented?

    i. Numbers or percentages?

    ii. What's the timeframe?

    iii. What are the details?

       1. Is it general, specific, jargon-y?

2. What are the implicit audience assumptions?

a. What kinds of things does the audience already assume are true? That is, what kind of interpretive model are they using?

Formatting and Data Type: It's important to remember that we all speak differently depending on the context of whom we are speaking to. We say things to our friends that we cannot say to our employers; we can say things to our significant others that we cannot say to a stranger. The fact of the matter is that the context of the audience completely alters what we say and how we say it.

Sometimes, the familiar words of ordinary speech take on a wholly different meaning when we're speaking to specific audiences. For example, "severe injury" means different things to different people – what is severe to you may be an ordinary injury to a surgeon. What is severe to the surgeon has much more severe implications for your health.

Formatting is about the style of presentation, e.g. in-depth, summary, narrative (a story), charts and graphs, etc. This tells us what kinds of expectations the author has regarding the audience, and what kinds of expectations we should have for the claim. If we're reading a narrative, we should not be expecting charts and graphs. If we're getting a summary, we can expect details to be omitted, etc.

When we see technical formatting, we should expect details, an in-depth explanation, a detailed justification, and citations - because that is what a technical claim requires. When we see a narrative, we should expect clear, non-technical language, and an overview of the situation. When you see a presentation for why a company should switch to using service X to save money, the details of the savings need to be precise, calculated, and well-justified. When I tell my friend a story about that presentation, I can say that we saved "a boatload of money."

Data type is about the kinds of information we are given. If you think back to the ways we can manipulate statistics, remember that the big difference showed up between total pay and percent of salary for the soccer teams. As a result, we need to pay attention to the kind of information we are (and are not) given. That tells us something about the audience, about the intention of the claim on that audience, etc. Are we seeing the whole picture? Which parts are pushed to the forefront, and which are omitted? This, again, goes to the kind of language that is used and the kind of specificity that language conveys.

The reason these details matter is because they influence how we interpret statements. Context determines whether the statements should be understood as literal or not, whether a phrase is a joke or an insult, whether the claim is adequately justified or not. As a general rule, the more casual a conversation, the less we expect the justification to be explicitly provided. You don't hold your friend's retelling of a funny moment in a movie to the same standards as you do a peer-reviewed article on the potentially lethal side-effects of a cancer treatment. The more serious the topic, the more details and justifications required. Exceptions exist, of course, as you would expect when Michael Che and Colin Jost (hosts of SNL's Week-end Update) cover that deadly cancer treatment story - because they are comedians.

If the formatting and content are out of sync – as happens if the topic is formal and serious, but the content is lacking in detail and justification - or vice versa – then we have a potential issue. Again, we note the issue, and account for it later.

You may be wondering: *what about claims without data?*

There is always data. Every claim is trying to tell you something. To do that, ideas and information must be presented. Ideas and information are data, whether they're presented as numbers, facts, and figures, or just as information about what is happening. Even missing information is still information – because now you can find out what's missing. That tells you 1) what you can go look up, and 2) what the audience is going to be assuming if they're accepting this claim.

For the second question - **what are the implicit audience assumptions?** - the assumptions of the audience are all about the kinds of things that are taken for granted. This includes the authoritative sources they do and do not consider valid, as well as what that validity means. For example, if we have a source on stock investment, those people who take the source as authoritative will buy when the source says to, and sell when it says to. For the people who consider the source as authoritative, they do not believe that they need to additionally verify the claims made by the authoritative source - because they have externalized and outsourced the expertise on that topic to that source. On the other hand, if I've never heard of the person giving the stock advice, I will need to verify who and what they are. That means that what Steve may assume is true (because of the source), I may not. The context of the audience makes a lot of difference in how we process claims.

As an easy example, we can think of a situation where a company is accused of some kind of wrongdoing. Now, imagine that we have two statements about the accusation, and both statements are from the CEO. One is a *public statement* issued by the company, the other one is a *leaked internal email*. If you had to pick one of these statements to bet on being the truth, without knowing what the statements actually said, which would you pick? Of course you would pick the internal email. Why? Because the audience goes from being a vague "general public" and shareholders, to a much more important figure of someone within the company. The difference in audience is what dictates whether the admission of wrongdoing is likely to be made, or how seriously we are going to take the denial of wrongdoing.

The question of the audience also ties in with the other speaker context elements. For example, the phrase "human nature is evil" means very different things depending on who the speaker is. More importantly, however, the phrase will mean very different things to different audiences. In Chinese, the word "evil" means something like, "*sub-par performance, given the resources and potential, within the context of the situation .*" If you miss the fact that the intended audience is Chinese, you might use a Western understanding of "evil" – something like, "hell-worthy trespass against the universal (natural, divine) law." At that point, you will miss the entirety of the meaning of the claim.[52]

Different audiences accept different ideas as true. That means that they require justification at different times, in different ways, and will accept or reject different arguments. By knowing the intended audience, we can find the kinds of hidden ideas that are at play, and whether they're being accepted or rejected. This gives us a more complete picture of the context that the claim is using for its justification.

---

52   This is a common issue with many students who read the classical Chinese text *Human Nature is Evil* by the classical Confucian scholar Xunzi (d. ~235 BC). The most common complaint is that the idea of humans as evil does not fit the students' ideas about human nature as derived from the Western, Judeo-Christian perspective. This is a rather silly complaint, because Xunzi is making a Chinese point about human nature and evil, not a Western one - and failing to catch the difference in the **meaning** of terminology then means that any counterargument fails, by default.

Finally, knowing the audience and the speaker allows us to start clarifying the intention of the speaker. As noted in the chapter covering context, Chris Rock and the DOJ spokesperson may address the same issue, but they do so in very different ways. However, Chris Rock is not always acting as a comedian, and the DOJ spokesperson is not always on the job. If Chris Rock is speaking to his children, or if he is (for some reason) testifying before Congress, we interpret his phrasing differently than we would if he were on stage. Similarly, if the DOJ spokesperson is talking to his buddy at a barbecue, we interpret the situation differently than we do when he is behind the official DOJ podium.

The difference is rather stark between an official comment and a joke, and between things said in public and private. Thus, we are able to gain an insight into the intention with which the speaker is acting. Of course, since we can't actually see intention, this is an approximation, but a rather useful one. This is how we can tell that Johnathan Swift's *A Modest Proposal* (1729) is satire and not an actual policy suggestion. Looking for this kind of insight also allows us to better keep our emotions in check; if we react to a joke, rather than respond to it, we are far more likely to get upset, outraged, etc., rather than realizing the joke for what it is.

The questions in this section have all been based on the context of audience point from Chapter 7. As with the speaker, we are expanding the questions to give ourselves more room for context, and reduce the chances of missing an important point. The audience and the speaker make up the conversation. We must know both, if we are going to make sense of the claim.

CASE STUDY

WHO IS THE AUDIENCE?

Turning back to our case study, we get to dig into Bloomberg, the story, and the audience.

When we ask about the **intended recipient of communication**, it can seem difficult with a newspaper. I mean, anyone can read it, right? That's true, but this kind of newspaper is not the Chicago Tribune or Washington Post (although, these also have their own targeted demographics). This is a business-oriented publication. How do we know? I didn't know until I googled it. Bloomberg Businessweek is targeted at the business/investment-oriented audience, who are non-experts on cybersecurity. This includes traders, investors, etc. who look to Bloomberg to give them insights, which they will convert into market activity.

What kind of formatting and data type are used in this story? Reading through the article (this is the first point where reading the article actually becomes necessary), we notice that the whole article is a narrative - a story. There are bits of jargon thrown in to spice it up, along with definitions for that jargon, but there is no data as such. Instead, what we see is claims made on the basis of sources that remain unnamed, and therefore unverified.

Finally, what kinds of implicit assumptions are in play here? What does the intended audience of Bloomberg Businessweek assume about the content? This might *seem* a bit difficult to discover at first, but with a bit of digging we can find an answer pretty easily - for our purposes. The Bloomberg audience accepts the authoritative status of Bloomberg on the topic of business-related content.

This means that they accept the authenticity and sincerity of anonymous sources, as long as they are presented by this kind of an authoritative outlet. We know this, because that's the style of writing that has been offered before by Bloomberg journalists (at least the ones we're looking at), without a problem - meaning that the Bloomberg audience has taken in that information and made business decisions on it. And, because the audience reacted by selling off Supermicro stock (as well as stocks of other named companies), we can additionally conclude that this is the case.

Although the length of this section may lead you to believe that this portion might not offer a lot of insight, the length of the answer changes from claim to claim. Here, we have concluded that the audience is a non-expert audience in cybersecurity, relying heavily (or even entirely) on an authoritative source for information, without critically examining the sources - because they believe the speaker's authoritative position. They will use that information to make business decisions. The speaker, for their part, offered the claim as a narrative without any data beyond the "I know a guy who knows things" role of the anonymous sources.

If we reflect on this summary, we can ask some questions:

- How do you feel about the answers about the audience?

- Have these answers made you feel better or worse about the issues raised about the speaker?

- Why? (be as specific as possible)

- How do you feel about the entirety of the claim now?

- If you were an investor (or just had money to invest), would you consider buying or selling Supermicro stock as a result of the story?

- Why? (be as specific as possible)

CHAPTER 14

METHODOLOGY (METRICS)

The third and last step in the Argument Buildup phase of the *Claim Shredder Method* is methodology. This is by far the most complex context you will have to navigate. Method is broken into two kinds: metrics and interpretation. These are two different sets of contexts, but they are based on the same issue – the methodology of how the claim is made. In the Argument Buildup phase, we deal with metrics. Here, we should remind ourselves of the three points made earlier: 1) all data is biased (because we have to make a selection based on relevance, and relevance is not a given); 2) there is an infinite number of interpretations for the same data (because data can be parsed in an infinite number of ways); and 3) the feature we're interested in is functionality - production of coherent, explanatory, actionable conclusions that fit our purposes.

Metrics asks three questions we must answer:

1. **What is being measured?**

2. **How is it being measured?**

3. Is it original or borrowed?

In case the claim is not relying on quantified/quantifiable factors, you can reformulate the questions as:

1. What is being claimed?

2. How is it being claimed/justified?

3. Is it original or borrowed?

The first two questions, in either formulation, happen in the context of the terms and definitions being used. This cannot be stressed enough: beware vague terms and definitions, and beware the statistics games.

Vague terms and definitions mean that we cannot actually determine the truth of a claim – because we have no idea what the claim is actually talking about. Imagine being presented with the following statement: "they are going to hack us!"

You can't agree or disagree with that statement, because you don't know who the "they" are, who the "us" are, or when the statement was made – so you don't know whether the issue is/was true or not; whether it has been resolved or not. Technically, you have a claim – but it is worded so vaguely that you can't do anything with it – at least not without getting a lot more context.

Let's look at a more critical example. The U.S. government uses predator drones to eliminate (kill) targets that present an "imminent threat" to the U.S. The traditional definition of "imminent threat" has been understood to mean that the threat was immediate (about to happen, right now), and that the person claiming that there is such a threat must be able to prove the threat and its immediacy by showing credible evidence of both. In analogous terms, if the average citizen uses deadly force and shoots someone, they would need to show that the person they shot was posing an immediate and clear threat to them – or they will be prosecuted for murder (at least that's the way it's supposed to work). That's because without this kind of "imminent threat" to their lives, they did not act in self-defense, they just shot a person on the street.

In 2011, the U.S. Department of Justice presented a **new definition** of "imminent threat" to justify actions like drone strikes that kill people abroad. The new definition says that: to consider something to "present an 'imminent' threat of violent attack against the United States *does not require the United States to have clear evidence that a specific attack on US persons and interests will take place in the immediate future* [emphasis added] (<u>US Department of Justice, 2011</u>: 7)."[53]

Notice that this new definition contradicts the original definition entirely. This leaves us with a very vague idea of what an imminent threat is supposed to be. If no evidence is needed, then anyone we don't like is, potentially, an imminent threat. All of a sudden, that term no longer means what it has meant for almost a century. If you don't catch the new vagueness in the term, you would be justified in believing that the "imminent threat" meant that we were about to get attacked, and just managed to stop it in time – even though that is no longer the meaning of the phrase as used by the DOJ.

We now see that the terminology must be concrete, or else we have no idea what the claim is actually saying. If we don't understand the claim clearly, we can't say the claim is good or bad – because we don't understand what the claim is. This connects us back to our discussion on *zhengming* and *wu-wei* of Chapter 10. As bad as vague terminology may be, things get worse with statistics.

Statistics games are deadly. We have already noted the various problems with statistics, but here I would like to demonstrate one of my favorites.

Dr. Steven Pinker makes the claim that humanity is getting less violent over time and that "we may be living in the most peaceful era in our species' history." (*Better Angels of Our Nature*).[54] Sounds great.

However, if that sounds a little funny to you, it should. Dr. Pinker provides a lot of data to prove his point, but that same data is where the problems lie.[55] For starters, he counts only the number of dead soldiers on the battlefield ("battle deaths"). This is problematic since fire-bombings, and other 20th century military tactics, are designed to obliterate civilian centers and civilians, not military targets and soldiers.

---

53   Badalic, Vasja. *The War Against Vague Threats. https://journals.sagepub.com/doi/full/10.1177/0967010620921006*

54   Pinker, Steven. *The Better Angels of Our Nature: Why Violence Has Declined.* Viking: New York; 2011. AND The University of Edinburgh. *Prof. Steven Pinker - The Better Angels of Our Nature: A History of Violence and Humanity.* https://youtu.be/o5X2-i_poNU

55   Herman, Edward S. and Peterson, David. *Steven Pinker on the alleged decline of violence.* https://isreview.org/issue/86/steven-pinker-alleged-decline-violence

Additionally, the major weapons developments in the 20th century have been aimed at large-scale destruction (which inherently includes civilian targets in the attacks), and the vast majority of war deaths in the 20th century were civilian deaths at the hands of militaries and paramilitary forces.[56] For reference, the 800,000 deaths in Rwanda in 1994 were effectively entirely civilian - not a single "battle death." The same is true for the genocide in Srebrenica in 1995. Yes, the 20th century was the least violent, if you don't count all the violence that happened.

Further, Dr. Pinker counts the dead not in total numbers, but as a percentage of the global population. For example, WWI cost 0.5% of the global population (9 million out of 1.7 billion total population at the time of WWI). The same casualties would now be understood as "better," because they would be 0.12% of the global population. The deaths and violence are the same, but the fact that we have a 440% population increase means that the deaths don't count as much. By that standard, the most murderous period ever in human history would have been the story of Cain and Abel - since the single murder was also the death of a huge percent of human population - a rather silly notion for a serious academic text. The book actually ended up with an entire issue of the *Historical Reflections* journal dedicated to debunking Dr. Pinker's thesis.[57]

Note that the problem here is not that Dr. Pinker is directly wrong. He does, in fact, have data that supports his conclusion. The issue, however, is the way that he seems to have selected and parsed through the data - effectively cherry-picking or warping statistics to prove his point, instead of seeing where it led.[58]

What about metrics in the case of a "claim" and "claim justification" version of this question? It seems relatively easy to point to metrics when we're dealing with quantifiable kinds of information, but what happens when the information is not quantifiable? Or, what happens when there is no quantification given?

---

56   Arquilla, John. *The Big Kill*. https://foreignpolicy.com/2012/12/03/the-big-kill/

57   Micale, M. S., & Dwyer, P. (2018). Introduction, Historical Reflections/Réflexions Historiques, 44(1), 1-5. https://www.berghahnjournals.com/view/journals/historical-reflections/44/1/historical-reflections.44.issue-1.xml

58   Epstein, Robert. Book Review: *The Better Angels of Our Nature: Why Violence Has Declined*. https://www.scientificamerican.com/article/bookreview-steven-pinker-the-better-angels-of-our-nature-why-violence-has-declined/

The thing to remember here is that metrics are not about quantification, but about definitions. Take, for example, the kinds of "lists" people make for the "top-5" in sports, music, etc. We can argue about these lists indefinitely – and it may be a lot of fun to do so. But what do we actually mean by something like "greatest basketball player?"

Can we include the now-retired or deceased players? Are we looking at the number of championships won? Total points scored? Highest points per game average? Rebounds? Triple-doubles? Are we accounting for the difference in how the game was played before, as opposed to how it is played now? Unless we decide what we mean by the phrase "the greatest," we can disagree forever, because we are never talking about the same thing. Bob is right because Michael Jordan has the most lifetime points, but Steve is also right because Dennis Rodman has the most rebounds in a game. They are talking right past each other.

The "greatest of all time" (G.O.A.T.) in rap is always an interesting discussion to listen to, because there is never a metric. Is it album sales? Radio-time? How often does it play at the club? Wealth of the rapper? It's fine to have your "list" made up of people you like the best – but in that case, that list is about preference, and your "claim" is just an emotional statement. It's no different than saying that your favorite ice cream flavor is pineapple. Strange choice, sure, but I can't argue with you about it (I can't tell you what your favorite flavor is), because it's a matter of preference - which is ultimately emotional.

Any claim at all is all about the definitions. Definitions are a way of recognizing some thing or some event or state of being. We need that definition so that we can check whether the thing we are seeing does or does not match that term. This is *zhengming* and *wu-wei* again. If it matches, we know what we're looking at. If it does not match, we at least know what we're not looking at. But if we assume that the terms and definitions of others mean what we think they mean, without checking, there is a very good chance that our understanding of what they say – and of what we are agreeing or disagreeing with – will be wrong.

Metrics (justifications) are the backbone of the claims we make. They are the "factual" basis for what we are working with. They are the justifying pyramid that gives us either a valid or invalid claim as a result. If the metrics go bad, it's a safe bet that everything depending on the metrics is going to fail pretty spectacularly as well.

Imagine the following lead up to a claim:

> *In order to understand the current state of state-sponsored cyber-attacks, we must remember that the Martian invasion of 1988 was thwarted by the United States, who discovered a great deal of advanced alien technology as a result.*

It sounds nice, but the fact that no such invasion happened means that any analysis building on this "data" is going to fail to provide anything resembling functional results.

So, if you get a claim without quantities, or without apparent metrics, just remember that you don't need quantities (unless you have a quantitative claim), and that metrics are hidden in the terms and definitions used. We actually don't care about numbers. We care about the structure that supports the claim.

To get at the metrics, we dig into the claim and its justification, and find the process by which the author is justifying the claim. It may be through numbers, it may be through arguments, it may be through history or through the claims of some other field of study. Whatever it is, we need to understand it, in order to make sure that the claim is actually resting on a solid foundation of justification.

The third question - **are the metrics original or borrowed?** - deals with the source of the metrics. This part inquires about the source of the data. Because metrics are critical to argument structure, we cannot merely assume that a cited paper or some such (regardless of the source) is valid. We cannot assume that the data or statistics borrowed from someone else are either accurate in the original source, or that they were accurately used by the present speaker, or that they are functional in this context. If any part of the core claim comes from another source, we have to go back to that source, and start the entire claim shredder process there again (starting with the author) - after we check that the source actually made the claim our speaker is referencing. That is, we must ensure that all elements important to the claim have been checked by us. In our pyramid visual, think of this process as checking the individual stones of the pyramid structure. Just because Bob says his claim works, does not mean that he is correct, nor does it mean that he has constructed the argument correctly. Check each "borrowed" stone.

On more than one occasion, we have discovered that reputable authoritative sources have used a common source of information to create their claims (a major paper, or "common knowledge" in their field). However, once we finally unearth that source – sometimes chasing the original through a dozen citations of separation – the originator of the claim might be estimating, flat-out guessing, or sometimes is an utterly incompetent, non-expert who is spouting clear nonsense. The thing is, when nonsense is presented the right way, it gets cited. Once it is cited, it takes on a life of its own. Very few authors who are farther down the chain will bother going back to check the original citation, and the garbage lives on.

As a secondary problem (this is why we first check that the supposed original source made the claim), false citations are used by some to lend an authoritative status to a would-be publication. The peer reviewers, even where competent, do not generally have the time to hunt down every single citation. That means that, if I want to make an unsupported claim, all I have to do is attribute it to an obscure (or even famous) source, and drop the fake justification in the footnotes. In plenty of academic disciplines, you will find that a citation hunt – the attempt to go back and cite the original paper – dead-ends. There is no such claim in that paper or on that page. Maybe the author misidentified the source, maybe they misquoted it, maybe there is no such source at all, maybe they accidentally wrote in the wrong source, maybe they did it intentionally. The point is, you cannot rely on the idea that information is published or cited as a form of verification. In fact, with some selective citing, one would be convinced that Iraq was behind the 9/11 attacks and was a major source of WMDs in the terrorist circles. Never mind that such a reading is wildly decontextualized and flat-out false. Anything I can get enough people to share, can take off and become a cited "fact."

Finally, the examination of metrics helps us further understand the motivations of the speaker. How so? There are two ways that claims are made:

1. Examine existing ideas → put them together → derive a new conclusion.

    a. This is the proper way to make a claim.

2. Pick a conclusion → find evidence to support the conclusion → arrange evidence so it looks like you took the first route.

The second way is the wrong way to go about making a claim. Why?

By deciding on the desired conclusion first, we become biased towards the kind of evidence and justification we're willing to consider. In effect, we go out cherry-picking only the data that supports our position, ignoring everything else. That means that the actual justification we present is decontextualized – not because we didn't know better, but because we didn't even want to look. Best case scenario, this is an issue of decontextualization by relevance (known-unknowns), though in many cases it is intentional and malicious.

When the justification provided in the metrics requires that we perform mental gymnastics to get it to fit the conclusion, we are forced to assume that the speaker had to go through that process as well. That means that the intent of the speaker was not to discover a truth by examining what is there, but to push a very specific interpretation onto the audience. In simpler English, that kind of a move is very suspicious.

We all have a sense of this "wrongness" about the claim, when we see just how badly one has to mangle the interpretation to make the claim work. Take the Dr. Pinker example above. As soon as you see just how much statistical squinting at the data he has to do to make his claim work, it becomes rather clear that he likely decided on the claim first, and then picked data until it seemed to back his position (why else would anyone decide to use such specific pieces of statistics, especially when the rates of violence have globally been directed at civilian, not military, targets?).

As a more common, everyday style misrepresentation, we've all seen the ads for some big sale, telling us that items are up to 75% off. Then, when we get to the store, we see that they have exactly one item that is 75% off, and everything else is 5% off (or has even been marked-up). Technically, the ad did not lie. Technically. But we all know the ad was essentially a scam to get people into the store.

When we see evidence of this kind of data manipulation, we learn something about the intent of the author. Either they are incompetent, or they are malicious. Either way, we have an issue we need to note and take into account in our final evaluation.

In this portion of the *Claim Shredder*, we are outlining the claim and the justification support structure, as well as defining terms. We are also linking the different pieces of support to their original sources, so that we end up with a layout (or a visual, if you're inclined to doodling) that shows us how these various pieces are supposed to fit together. This gives us a roadmap of the work we will do in phase 2 of the *Claim Shredder*, in order to arrive at our conclusion.

This portion is also the most difficult for many students, because it is research heavy. Because of data bias and infinite interpretations, we are forced to go through the claim and its justification and confirm each and every term used. We cannot assume anything. And very often, the devil is exactly in these details. However, as you get more used to the process, you will find that the research gets easier. Once you get into the habit of asking the questions, you will get into the habit of looking up the definitions without thinking twice. Thankfully, access to the internet makes a lot of this work rather simple, if repetitive.

CASE STUDY
METHODOLOGY (METRICS)

Let's return to our case study, and see how well it does in this section.

What is being measured/claimed?

Jordan Robertson is claiming that a number of major US companies (everyone using Supermicro motherboards) have been compromised by a Chinese hardware hack. [A hardware hack is a hack, but instead of malware or a virus, it is your physical components of your computers/servers that are at issue].

How is this being measured/how is the claim justified?

Jordan Robertson tells us that the chip is real (that's the part that does the hacking), and that apparently the mere presence of that chip means that you are hacked. That is, no degree of security means anything if you have one of the compromised motherboards. What that means, and this is where the claim takes on additionally fantastical proportions, is that even air-gapped systems are compromised, and the Chinese government knows what's happening on those machines ("air-gap" refers to computers, etc. that are not connected to anything - no internet, no Bluetooth, no connection to the outside world at all - which is the way that organizations like the CIA operate).

Let's say we are willing to believe that. What's the justification for this claim?

Here, we hit a pretty big wall. Jordan Robertson does not offer any data, or any real justification at all. What he does give us is mostly anonymous sources. The few named sources, like Joe Grand - apparently the leading US expert on hardware hacking (I googled him and found out)

- explicitly refute the possibility of such a hack. In an interview a few weeks later, Joe Grand said, "I've never personally seen real-world hardware implants."[59]

Entities named in the story, including the Department of Homeland Security, GCHQ (Government Communications Headquarters - UK agency), Amazon, Apple, Supermicro, etc. all denied the story.

The claim made by Jordan Robertson is a massive one. Not only are top US companies affected, so is the US government, and others. And, crucially, there is a way to bypass all of our security measures (which would be the top security story in the last few decades, even if we take the Chinese government and hacking out of the story). The problem, however, is that this massive claim is lacking in the metrics department. All we have is the word of a non-expert journalist, who is relying on anonymous sources for the entirety of his story. This is why the lack of expertise and a lack of transparency are such a bad combination: we have no way of verifying any of the claims made, and they are not trivial claims. There is no decent way to confirm the **how** part of the metrics so far.

But, who knows? Maybe there is enough evidence to make the claim work elsewhere.

For right now, the speaker is a bit suspicious, the audience is not the greatest (in inspiring us to jump on board with the claim), and the metrics are seriously iffy.

---

59   Joe Grand. Interview with *The Security Ledger*. 10/9/2018. https://securityledger.com/2018/10/podcast-episode-115-joe-grand-on-unicorn-spotting-and-bloombergs-supply-chain-story/

CHAPTER 15

METHODOLOGY (INTERPRETATIONS)

Interpretations are phase 2 of the *Claim Shredder Method*; at the end of which we will make our decision on the validity of the claim in question. As we have noted earlier, interpretive models play an important role in how the claim is understood.

There are a few assumptions that we need to make and reiterate, before we get to the questions themselves. The first of these, as before, is to assume that the claim is something valuable. That is, we want to assume that the claim contains something that we want to get out of it. The reason why we make this assumption is in order to fight our own biases and preconceived notions. Thus, we assume the claim has value, so that we'll try everything we can to extract value out of it.

The good news is that, whether the claim is true or false, we can still get something of value out of it – if we try our best. Even false claims tell us something. For example, examining a false claim teaches us what does not work. More importantly, we can understand why a claim like this does not work and we may come to understand why the claim in question seemed like a good idea to the person who proposed it. That means that we get to identify a pattern of thinking which leads to bad answers. Once we see the way these kinds of patterns work (or rather, fail to work), we can learn to identify them quickly, and make these kinds of judgments faster. We can also make sure that our thinking does not fall into any of these failed patterns.

The second assumption we need to make is that we are ignorant about some crucial element of this claim. That is why we are asking these questions to begin with. If we already knew everything, there would be no reason to ask questions, and we would already know whether the claim was valid or not. If, instead, we assume that we are ignorant, we start to ask these questions in earnest i.e. in good faith and with sincerity, because we truly want to know the answer(s). This allows us to engage in the proper style of *wu-wei* – observing what the thing is instead of trying to force it to be something that fits our preconceived notions.

Why does this matter?

When we engage with a new idea based on our preconceived notions, we tend to be wrong more often than not. That is, some part of what we assume we know is wrong, and/or some part of how we assume the claim is supposed to work is wrong. Since our job is to determine the truth of this specific claim, preconceived notions about the claim are a bad way to do our job. Relying on preconceived notions is a good way to properly stereotype things we already know, and it is the main way that we react. As noted, a new claim is a thing we don't already know, and reactions are not what we're after. Since we're trying to respond, we have to put our reactions (and assumptions) aside, and really engage with the claim itself.

As we shift into the methodology of interpretation, we are going to ask three sets of questions.

1. Clarification questions

2. Conditional Questions

3. Questions of evidence

At the end of this process, we will understand the claim, understand the implications of the claim, and arrive at the conclusion about the claim. At that point, we will have a fully formed opinion, based on the best critical thinking and analysis, and will be able to say whether the claim is true or false.

If these question sets look familiar, they should. They came up back in Chapter 9. All we are doing here is articulating them a bit further, to give ourselves more room for gathering additional context.

CHAPTER 16

QUESTIONS OF CLARIFICATION

Clarification questions are intended to ensure that we have fully understood the claim as it is presented. If we misinterpret a claim, any conclusions about its validity become unreliable. Part of this process, as you will see, is also intended to ensure that the previous questions have been satisfactorily answered, and to expand on their context - so that we may end up with a complete picture. There are four clarification questions:

1. What do you mean by that?

Here, we try to make sure that we're getting the overall meaning of the idea/claim. We do that by turning the whole idea into a 1-3 sentence executive summary. It takes actual understanding of the idea/claim to break it down to an executive summary. If you can't summarize the whole thing in 1-3 sentences, go back and try summarizing smaller pieces first, and then fitting them together. One highly effective tactic is to write out a short, 1-sentence summary of each paragraph as you read. That allows you to look back and see how the idea is structured, and also to find key points, which you can then turn into a summary of the claim as a whole.

For dealing with a text, a good approach is to write down your summary of it, and then check to see whether your summary is contradicted by any point of the text. For in-person questions, a great approach is to ask the question in reverse: "I want to make sure I understand this right. Are you saying that [insert your executive summary]?"

This kind of phrasing is important when engaging another person, because it: A) tells the other person that you're actively paying attention and trying to comprehend the claim, and B) it gives the other side a chance to correct your understanding or add any other points they consider important to the claim.

It is critical to watch for word choice and make sure you get it right. A single wrong word can un-make the argument. Words have meaning, but they also have implications. We use implications of words in order to navigate language, to figure out what the speaker is trying to communicate. When a speaker picks a word with the wrong implication, they communicate the wrong idea.

For example, one of the Ten Commandments is commonly translated as "Thou shall not kill." However, let's consider the meaning that phrase can and cannot have: In order to live, we have to kill things. We kill, one way or another, because we run on bio-chemical energy, which we can't produce on our own - since we're not able to photosynthesize. We kill animals for food, we kill plants for food, we kill all sorts of microbial life just in the process of eating. And that's fine, because killing is simply the ending of life. To kill is to end a life – the term is not morally laden. On the other hand, murder can be better understood as the intentional, unjustified, and (by-definition) unjust taking of human life.

Note the issue that arises here. If we take the commandment to be "Thou shall not <u>kill</u>," we have a problem. We have to kill to survive – whether you're killing animals, vegetables, fruit, insects, or microbes. And if you don't kill, then you can't eat - and not eating means that you are killing yourself. Now you have a paradox: no matter what you do, you're killing something – either by surviving or by dying. By contrast, you don't have to murder. Therefore, we can conclude that (no matter the translation) the functional, non-contradictory version of the commandment actually means "Thou shalt not murder."

Getting the phrasing right, understanding the meaning intended correctly, and communicating in an articulate way yourself, is critical to understand the claim.

2. Can you say that in a different way?

Blindly parroting the same words back, without any understanding is easy. In fact, I am sure you have seen political talking points that are just repeated in the exact same way, even when the speaker is asked to elaborate on the point. That's a hallmark of parroting an idea.

Trying to explain the idea in a new way - i.e. rephrasing an idea – requires us to first grasp it fully. If you cannot do this, you are missing key points of the claim. It is possible that there is nothing there to be understood, because the claim is not really a claim – it is just a word salad. We have to assume that there is some point to the claim, if we are trying to be charitable. Only if we can't make any sense of it at all – no matter how charitably we read – are we allowed to conclude that this is a word salad.

When we understand the meaning of the idea, we can easily rephrase it. This is because rephrasing is a matter of using different words to communicate the same underlying concept. So, to borrow from the commandment example above, we can rephrase the commandment as "no person is allowed to intentionally and unjustly take the life of another person." We could also rephrase that as "taking the life of another person can only be carried out if justice demands it (that is, justly)." We can keep on rephrasing, because we understand what the point of the commandment is, so finding multiple ways of saying the same thing is easy.

However, if we don't understand the underlying meaning of the claim, then we have nothing to work with. If we don't understand the point of what is said, the claim itself is just noise to us; therefore, we cannot use a different set of words to communicate the same idea, because we don't know what the idea is. When a claim is a word salad, there is nothing for us to understand. When there is no underlying meaning there; there is no way to rephrase.

Here's a quick example: *do you agree that dkjbgfpiyg is good for your health?*

That key term in that statement is just button-mashing on a keyboard. There is nothing there to understand. Since you cannot understand the key point to the question, you can't meaningfully answer.

You might have had this experience in other situations, like math or physics – that is, in places where we tend to memorize formulas of some kind. So long as the problem you get is exactly what you practiced on, you know how to plug it into the formula. But if the situation changes, suddenly you don't know what to do. People who actually understand the subject don't have to memorize formulas; they understand the problem and can derive the formulas as needed. Similarly, understanding the claim lets you derive different ways of communicating the same ideas.

3. Can you give an example?

The purpose of this question comes from the fact that examples are the most simple – and often the most effective – way of communicating an idea. If you cannot give an example of the claim, even a hypothetical one, either you have not grasped it properly, or there is nothing to be grasped.

If you look at the various ideas we've covered throughout this book, you will notice that there are a lot of examples. In fact, this paragraph here is an example. This is intentional: if you don't understand the more technical language, or if it is not clear in that technical language, the examples give you a practical way of wrapping your head around the idea. This is also why using multiple and varied examples can be useful. If your audience does not understand a point you make with an example from linguistics, they might understand it through math – or through some other field of study or personal experience.

If there is no example you can find of the claim, and no example you can come up with, you might be looking at nonsense. Even in purely theoretical fields, where there is nothing physical to interact with, we can give examples. Science fiction and fantasy books are exercises in creating examples out of imaginary concepts. If you can give an example about Hobbits – things that literally do not exist – then you should be able to give an example of anything else that you understand.

4. Why do you think that?

The final question on clarification is also the most complex. When we ask "why?" we are looking for a rational justification, based on rational premises. When we apply this question in the Claim Shredder, we are looking for two distinct points:

1. What data, and what chain of logical connections between that data, have led the speaker

to their conclusion?

2. Where did the data come from?

The first part is something like an executive summary of the executive summary, focused solely on the structure of the argument. What information is the speaker using? How is it arranged? What is the conclusion? This is the pyramid part of our visual from Chapter 3.

The second part should look familiar. It was the third question in Chapter 14. We are listing the question here again, because it bears repeating, and is possibly the most common source of our own failure to properly engage in critical thinking. If we don't know where the data came from, we don't know anything about it, and we can't reasonably discern whether it is functional for our purposes or not, or whether it is even true. Take the time to check the sources – always.

You'll notice that the clarification questions articulate the key points of the claim, but they also go a long way toward revealing the structure of what's going on. Once you see where the ideas are coming from, how they're tied together, and the justification for the interpretation offered, you can see how the ideas of the claim are actually coming together into a single edifice. This is like a single structure designed to use the foundations and the base to make its point at the top.

Quite often, the major objection on this point is that, "this takes too long!" In a way, that objection is right: it does take a long time to do all this checking and double-checking of everything that is said, of who said it, etc. However, the question we should ask in response to this objection is: **what is the alternative?**

If we accept a single piece of bad information, everything else that we build on top of that information is now insufficiently justified. Every conclusion we draw is now suspect. Every other claim that relates to this one, and relies on it being true, is now bad as well. That entire cascade of failure is caused by a single piece of bad information. Here's a useful way of thinking about this issue:

It is better to have one piece of information that we are certain about, than a hundred pieces that are questionable.

When we have certainty in our information, we can work with it, and build on it, knowing that it will hold up. Questionable information is always doubtful; it can fall apart at any moment and take down everything related to it as well. Think of this in terms of climbing: would you rather climb up to a roof slowly but be sure that you will not fall, or would you prefer to climb quickly up a rickety ladder that may break at any moment – leaving you with a broken back? To be sure, if you're getting chased by a bear, you want to climb quickly – even if it is very risky. This is because the bear is a far greater risk and you are certain that the bear will turn you into dinner. But imagine that your job is to climb up on roofs all day, every day. Not once, but thousands of times. All of a sudden, you need that climb to be as safe as possible, because any risk – multiplied thousands of times – becomes a near-certainty down the line. Sure it's slower, but you won't be ending up with a broken back.

Since we take in thousands of pieces of information every day, and make thousands of decisions based on that information every day, it is crucial that our information is right (or at least as right as we can get it to be). Even if that means that you can only read one new thing a day (but read it carefully), it is far better than reading all the things and having no idea what's true and what's false. This is because your ability to make good, functional choices, that get you what you want, depends on having accurate information – not a lot of iffy information.

Once you have answered the questions of clarification, and put them together with phase 1 of the *Claim Shredder*, you should have a complete grasp on the claim. You have checked, and checked again, to ensure that you are not misinterpreting the idea, that your understanding is not skewed, that you are approaching the claim as rationally as possible. That places you in an excellent position to engage with the meaning and implications of the claim - which is precisely what we will do next.

CASE STUDY

QUESTIONS OF CLARIFICATION

Going back to *The Big Hack*, we can ask the clarification questions there to see what we get.

What do you mean by that?

Going off the article, what Jordan Robertson means is that:

The Chinese government backdoored computer hardware, in a never-before-seen hardware implant hack, bypassed all security measures, and gained access and information to all infected computers, by compromising Supermicro motherboards.

We are sure that this is what is meant, since this is a summary of the article. In fact, if you take a look at several follow-up articles published by Jordan Robertson, they confirm this reading of the original.

Can we say that in a different way?

Since the claim is pretty well laid out, yes we can. For example, if asked to rephrase the claim, we can turn it into something like this:

Supermicro motherboards, used by the U.S. government and major U.S. corporations, were compromised at their point of creation by the Chinese government - which used this physical hack/compromise to gain access to and information from the users of the affected motherboards. Pretty straightforward, right?

Is there an example?

Unfortunately, there are no examples given anywhere in the article. There is no justification given that can be independently verified. The entire thing hinges on anonymous sources presented as "trust them, they are legit."

Why does the speaker believe the claim/why should we?

The speaker tells us that he believes the claim on the basis of his anonymous sources. If they showed him any information to help him believe it, he has not shared that information with us. The article takes the position that we (the audience) should believe the claim on the basis of the fact that an authoritative source (Bloomberg) has said so, and the best we can get is that Bloomberg journalists believe their own sources - which are not named and cannot be verified by us.

You should note here that we just found an interesting implication. Although we will get to the implications in the next chapter, we will pause here to explain the process a bit. If the speaker believes the claim based on his sources, then either they showed him information to make him believe, or they did not. How and why would you trust a source making a big claim, if they did not show you proof? Because of **who** the source is - they would have to be incredibly trustworthy in some way. So, now we know that the implication here is that either the speaker was given information to make him believe the claim (which he then failed to share with his readers), or his sources are so trustworthy that they don't need to show him evidence for him to believe them. That second option is a problem, because his sources are anonymous to us, so we have no clue whether they actually are that trustworthy. You should be able to see how the question of the speaker is now affecting the clarification of the claim and its justification.

Now that we have a clear grasp on the claim itself, we can ask some questions:
- Has clarifying the claim and its justification made you feel better or worse about the claim?
- Why? (be as specific as possible)
- If you were asked to justify your "feeling" about the claim, could you point to clear points of strength/weakness?
- What kind of evidence would it take for you to change your opinion?
- Do you think that it is likely that such evidence exists?
- Why do you think so? (be as specific as possible)

CHAPTER 17

CONDITIONAL QUESTIONS

Conditional questions, just like conditionals in logic and programming, are "if-then" statements. In the previous section, we asked questions to make sure we understand what the claim means and how it was put together. In this section, we are asking about the implications, limits, and the rules and exceptions - as defined in Chapter 9. These questions should allow us to understand the meaning of the claim. Notice also that we can't meaningfully do this part of critical thinking until we have a solid grasp on the claim itself; if we don't understand the claim, we can't work out its meaning, implications, etc.

Onto the questions themselves:

1. Can you think of a case where the claim is not true?

If you can find so much as a single counterexample, it means that the claim is not absolute, or not as generalized as the speaker made it out to be (whether they're presenting it as a rule or an exception). That is, in the best-case scenario for the claim, it is actually limited to some less general conditions than what the speaker presented. These limits must be met to make the claim functional. It is also possible that a counterexample means that the claim/idea is entirely false, but we should not assume that. Instead, assume that there are some kinds of limits on the idea, then try to see what the limits are. If you can't make it work with any limits, then it is likely to be false.

Often, people make absolute claims, intending to or not, which makes counterexamples easy. Since we're looking to do charitable reading, and not to troll, we can assume that – unless the whole claim hinges on the absolute nature of the claim, it may have been intended as a non-absolute. Therefore, we go looking for the limits.

Let's look at an example:

"Slavery is a moral evil." That statement seems really straightforward. When we hear the term "slavery," most of us immediately associate it with the North Atlantic slave trade (Middle Passage), and all the horrors that period produced. And so, it seems like this statement is true. However, can I think of an example where this statement is not true? Yes, I can – though probably not in the way you think.

The term slavery/slave is a fairly universal – as in, most every society ever has had the idea. However, what that idea means is not at all the same across these societies. While we're used to thinking of slavery as a terrible moral evil, the Chinese version of the idea was completely different. First, it had nothing to do with owning people (the Chinese language can't even make sense of that idea – you can own objects, and since people are not objects, they can't be owned). Second, slavery in China had nothing to do with hard labor. Third, it had nothing to do with being deprived of rights or treated poorly. Instead, the classical Chinese idea of slavery was associated with being a servant to the empire – becoming a public official, whose purpose was to work for the benefit of the state, not for personal profit. These were prestigious positions, and families spent generations trying to become the kinds of people who would be accepted as slaves.[60]

Clearly, then, there is at least one counterexample.

You might be wondering where we went wrong with the initial statement? As in the example of "Religion causes wars," we have an unlimited statement – "slavery" – which becomes an absolute term

---

60   For a great article on this issue, see: https://yaqeeninstitute.org/abdullah-hamid/slavery-and-islam-what-is-slavery

(any behavior that was described as "slavery"). And, just as with our examples of *zhengming* and *wu-wei*, we made a bad assumption that the term had only one possible meaning. What we probably understood when we read that statement is, *"the kind of slavery that was present in the North Atlantic slave trade is a moral evil."* And that statement is a pretty solid one. Notice that all we did here was apply a limit on the original statement. That limit keeps us from bringing up the Chinese idea of slavery, because that's not what the speaker wanted to include.

This is also why we want to read charitably. How many people reading this are at all aware of the variations in the meaning of the idea of slavery? Probably very few. Therefore, we assume that the speaker was probably limited in their understanding of the idea, and we apply the limit of only certain kinds of slavery, to try to get a functional claim. If the claim's conclusion is about why, "ending the North Atlantic slavery trade was a morally good idea," the absolute nature of the claim is not a problem. That is because the speaker seems to be dealing not with slavery as a universal concept, but with a particular instance of that slavery. When we limit the meaning of the statement to that particular instance of slavery, we can make the whole claim make sense. But, if the conclusion is something like, "every society that supported slavery is an evil society," then our counterexample can sink the claim.

That said, we still note the potential weakness that is created by the absolute term, so that we can address it later on.

2. If the claim is true, what else must be true?

This is a key question for taking claims apart. You start by assuming the truth of the claim, and then looking for other bits of truth that must accompany it. The fact of the matter is, a lot of data in many claims (think science studies that require CERN-level technology) cannot be easily replicated or directly tested. When we know what else we should be seeing as a result, we can often track those secondary effects much more easily.

For example, let's take the claim that "abortion ought to be legal because of rape and incest cases." Here we have an unlimited term - abortion - which is going to make this a claim about the general legalization of abortion, not an exceptional set of cases. As a result, it must be true that the rate of women seeking abortions for rape and incest cases justifies making abortion generally legal. What we would expect to see, then, is that the number of women seeking abortions for these reasons will be a sizable portion of all abortions; that is, it must be true that the rape and incest cases are fairly prevalent reasons for abortions. If it turns out that this reason makes up less than 2% of why abortions are sought,[61] then we have a problem: the claim is overly generalized, and is trying to use an exception to create a general rule. This would make the claim very weak, because (as noted in chapter 9) we don't make general rules based on exceptions.

Notice that this is not an argument about whether abortions are morally permissible, or whether they should or should not be legal for any other reason. The claim above is structured specifically on the idea of a rule - not the exception to the rule - because it is seeking general legalization of abortion, not exceptional case legalization. That means that, according to the claim, it's not good enough to make abortions legal for rape and incest cases as an exception to the rule.

Pop-quiz: We already noted that topics like abortion tend to cause reactions in people. That's why this example was chosen here. Did you respond or react to this example?

3. If the claim is true, what cannot be true?

This is a complimentary question to the previous one. Again, we are assuming the truth of the claim as a starting point, and then looking to see whether the things that cannot be true are actually present. Again, we do this for the same reason – ease of access to secondary data, allowing for verification by implication.

Although the goal is the same as the previous question, we want to ask this as a separate question to make sure that we turn our attention to both what we should and should not be finding. This is a way of making sure that we don't miss any relevant ideas.

Again, as with the previous question, the contradiction is not proof that the claim is garbage, but is it a definite proof that, at best, the claim is more limited than the original claim suggests. One good way of approaching these two questions is to try to flip the phrasing of the answer. That is, if something (X) must be true, then we can say that "it can't be true that X is false."

---

61   According to the Guttmacher institute, rape and incest cases are less than 1.5% of reasons why abortions are sought in the US. https://www.guttmacher.org/sites/default/files/pdfs/pubs/psrh/full/3711005.pdf Pg. 113.

The reason for these questions is to build up some context around the claim itself. We're assuming that the claim is true for all three questions. That is, we're not trying to deny the claim, but are trying to explore it. This, as you may recall, is the key feature of our earlier discussion of reaction vs. response. Instead of trying to attack the claim, we grant it conditional legitimacy (assume it is true, so we can test it), in order to follow its train of thought. Far more often, this approach allows us to find the faults in the claim more effectively than attacking it directly would. Additionally, the approach shows us how and where to use the two important features we noted in Chapter 6 - namely, the claim's internal coherence, and its external coherence.

As we ask the conditional questions, we are measuring the claim against its own understanding of the world. That will tell us, in the next part, how and why the author interprets the world in a way that supports their claim. At this point, you should have a clear understanding of how the claim is structuring reality, what is being included and excluded, how the claim is and is not limited, and what it all means. Examining a claim in this way will expose any weaknesses and inconsistencies lurking in the claim, which will allow us to take the very last step in determining whether a claim is valid or not.

CASE STUDY
CONDITIONAL QUESTIONS

It's time to ask some conditional questions of our case study article.

Is there a case where the claim is not true?

There seems to be a lot of those cases, because every entity named in the article denies the claim - Supermicro, Apple, Amazon, DHS, etc. However, according to the speaker, his anonymous sources also come from those same organizations that are denying the story. As we noted a few chapters back, official statements are less trustworthy than inside information. So, despite the fact that we have a lot of companies, organizations, and even governments denying the claim, that does not seem to give us an open-and-shut case where the claim is not true.

If the claim is true, what else must be true?

The way I approached this section was to break down the story into several sections, about a paragraph long each, and then write out a sentence that would summarize the paragraph. That summary is what the speaker is telling us is true. Then, I sat back and thought about the kinds of necessary conditions for that statement to be true - or what else could not be true.

1.   **It must be true** that a thing never done before (hardware implant hack), was done at scale, and was executed flawlessly. [Anyone who might be into anything related to computer science knows that there is no such thing as flawless execution, especially not the first time] **How I got to this point:** Our experts say they have never seen such a thing before; China has not only seen it, they built it, installed it, and ran it undetected for years (according to the article).

2.   Also, according to the story, the tools and manpower involved in the detection and

investigation of the hack were massive. Half of the U.S. alphabet soup agencies (FBI, CIA, DHS, etc.) were involved. That's not to mention all the corporate players who were mixed up in it as well. And yet, somehow, despite all the people, there has not been a single leak about the issue anywhere at all. And then, in order for the story to work, **it must be true** that a whole lot of people with classified information on the case suddenly decided to speak, all at once, to some Bloomberg journalist you have never heard of before - ever. **How I got to this point:** The story names the many alphabet soup agencies involved in detection and investigation; this is the first story on the topic, so there must not have been any other leaks; the story claims that there are anonymous sources from a lot of the companies and agencies who spoke to the journalist; the two journalists are relative unknowns.

3.   Additionally, **it must be true** that the same anonymous sources who spoke with Jordan Robertson chose a no-name journalist over, say, Wikileaks. In fact, they chose him over other major journalists who have been very influential in working with the cybersecurity world and U.S. government misdeeds, and exposing meaningful information (Glenn Greenwald, for example, was the point of contact for Snowden; Jeremy Scahill wrote *Dirty Wars*). **How I got to this point:** Again, the two Bloomberg journalists are unknowns - meaning that there is no history of them doing such massive stories right - and you want to get something like this right.

4.   If the claim about the sources is true, then the act of speaking about the ongoing government investigation into the hack compromises that investigation. Therefore, **it must be true** that the sources would intentionally be harming their own investigation of a foreign government hacking the U.S. government, companies, and individuals. **How I got to this point:** Talking to the public about secret ongoing investigations lets the other side know you're onto them and gives them time to cover things up; more coverups mean more difficult time investigating.

5.   Further, **it must be true** that the act of such disclosure means a complete disregard for all security/classified clearance oaths by the sources. This is an act of treason.

How I got to this point: If the U.S. government is keeping the investigation under wraps, everyone working on it has a non-disclosure agreement (NDA) and the information is classified. Speaking to a journalist violates the NDA and classified information access. Intentionally revealing classified information is an act of treason.

6.   Finally, it **must be true** that the people we hold to be top experts (like the aforementioned Joe Grand) are completely uninformed about the state of their own field of expertise. **How I got to this point:** The expert says this has never been done before and is impossible; the story says the impossible was done. If the story is true, the expert is not an expert. If the expert is right, the story is garbage.

If the claim is true, what can't be true?

1.   **It can't be true** that the sources are engaging in this disclosure for "patriotic" reasons - as was the case for Manning or Snowden (whether you believe their actions are actually patriotic or not is irrelevant; they seemed to have come from a patriotic place). In the case of Manning and Snowden, they believed that there was a U.S. government conspiracy to engage in actions that were unconstitutional, and to hide the truth from the U.S. citizens. Thus, they spoke out to bring this information to light and let the U.S. citizens know what their government was doing illegally. **How I got to this point:** In *The Big Hack* case, the U.S. government is trying to fix a dangerous situation, and is engaged fully in the investigation of that situation, and is doing pretty well at it. By speaking publicly about the investigation, the sources compromise its functionality.

2.   As a result, **it can't be true** that this leak is a coherent means of doing anything other than harming the investigation. This means that we have to conclude that the anonymous sources would be committing treason without reason. **How I got to this point:** I added up the previous points about compromising investigation, and about such compromise not being at all helpful to the general public.

Internal and External Coherence

As we read through the claim, we start noticing that there are parts of the story that don't seem to add up here. Besides the aforementioned issues (we're stopping at 8 for the sake of space), we also have other parts of the article that make little sense in their own right.

For example: at one point, Jordan Robertson tells us that, after the hack was detected, the U.S. government agencies carried out a secret mission in China and saw the Chinese government official pressure the local Supermicro factory into installing the hardware hack. At the same time, Jordan Robertson tells us that the hack (and presumably the pressuring of the manufacturer by the government) happened 2.5 years before anyone in the U.S. detected it or looked for it. Also, it's not a new factory, but the same one that had been doing the work already.

What we have here is internal incoherence - two or more ideas that are both claimed to be true, but which prevent each other from being true. If the Chinese government finished forcing manufacturers to install the chips 2.5 years before the hack was detected, then how did the investigators witness them doing it (live and in person) 2.5 years later? If the story is true, then either the U.S. government has invented time travel (nope), or the Chinese government reenacts the "pressure manufacturer" bit every year - like some sort of a weird ritual (again, no).

Going all the way back to our issue with the speaker, we can work through a different chain of implications. As mentioned in the previous case study section, if the story is true, then the speaker believes it is true. So, the speaker must have had enough evidence to be convinced that the story is true. What convinced him? What piece of information or argument was good enough to take a story like this, and make him believe it - and believe it enough that he wrote the article? Either he saw some information that proved it to him, or he believes his sources. Presumably, because of the co-author, whatever convinced one person also had to convince the other. So, what is it?

If it was information he saw, has he shared that information with his audience? No, he has not. That makes his own article much weaker. If he had information, why not share it and show us why he believes the story? How can we verify his story without information? If he believes his sources because he knows them (or they are incredibly highly placed), then how can we believe the story unless we know who the sources are? At best, we can conclude that he trusts his sources, but that does nothing for us (we cannot know the functionality of the information or the sources).

On top of that, the journalistic standard is to **lead** with the point that convinced the journalist, because that kind of information is what is expected to convince the reader as well. If a story claims that Chicago had 769 homicides and a surge in gun violence in 2020, the story will start with the source of that information, like this:

CHICAGO (AP) — The number of homicides and shootings in Chicago spiked dramatically in 2020, ending with more bloodshed than in all but one year in more than two decades, statistics released by police on Friday revealed.

The fact that we're missing the "reason to believe this story" point, is making the claim weaker and the kind of evidence we need a lot higher.

As we dig into the claim, the story itself starts to lose cohesion and come apart at the seams.

CHAPTER 18

QUESTIONS OF EVIDENCE

As the final set of questions, we need to consider the evidence for the claim. As noted in Chapter 9, the questions of evidence require us to ask them in a specific order, so as to avoid polluting the answer with our own biases. Commonly, when we have a preference for an answer about the claim, we tend to change our standards on evidence. This is because we have an agenda and we're trying to make our ideas work – whether they actually work or not.

For example, when we want something to be true, our requirements for evidence suddenly drop. Any evidence at all, no matter how bad, is good enough, because it supports something we want. On the other hand, when we don't like an idea, suddenly no evidence is good enough. Whatever evidence we get, we still have "questions." We call this the "moving the goalposts" fallacy. However, if we approach the questions of evidence in the right order, we can minimize the risk of this problem.

Make sure you write down your answers to these questions, because that tactic helps us get a better view – a more objective understanding – of the questions and our answers to them.

1. What kind of evidence do we need to back up this claim?

In light of the preceding questions and the answers we have derived, and the kinds of problems that have arisen that we have to account for, we ask what kind of evidence would be sufficient to make the claim valid and trustworthy? What kind of evidence could override any concerns raised thus far? This should be noted down and clearly defined. Additionally, we must justify for which purpose which piece of evidence is needed and why.

At this point, we start looking back to all those issues we noted needed to be accounted for. From the speaker to the audience, metrics, etc. every point that raised an issue now has to be ironed out. When we are asking for evidence needed to back up a claim, we are asking *what would it take to make this claim rationally acceptable, despite all the issues so far*? Making a note of all the issues as we go along allows us to see that full list at the end of the process, and to have a clear overview of the part of the claim that has to be additionally justified.

As an added benefit, with a list of possible problems in hand, it is easier to see if the same piece of evidence might resolve several problems at once. The more such combined pieces of evidence we can identify, the easier the next question becomes.

You can think of the process so far in terms of baking a cake:

You went through the recipe (claim) and then through your cupboard. If you have all the ingredients, you can start baking (fully justified claim). But, if you have ingredients missing (issues you must account for, because the proper justification is missing), you have to make a list of what you're missing (what evidence do we need?), and then go see whether you can get those ingredients elsewhere (what evidence do we have?).

2. What kind of evidence do we have?

Once the evidence requirements are clearly defined, we then ask what kind of evidence is available. The first step in evidence collection is to work strictly from the text itself. That is, try to see if there are explanations in the text that will give you enough evidence. If that's not enough, then we have to start additional research – asking questions like, "*is there another article/claim by the same speaker that would explain the problem here?"* Sometimes, speakers have defined their terms three articles ago, so you have to go back to get the information. This is also why we ask questions about who the speaker is - because it gives us insight into other things they may have said/done/published that we can draw on later. Once you have all the evidence requirements listed side by side with what evidence is available, you can see how the two match up. You can also clearly see where the required evidence is missing, and so on.

In our baking example, when we have a list of the ingredients we need to make the claim work, it is fairly easy to compare it with the kind of ingredients (evidence) we have and see where we might have missing ingredients. It is also much more difficult to convince yourself (or anyone else) that you have all the ingredients, when the two lists clearly don't match up.

3. Possibility v. Plausibility:

Here, we have to remind ourselves of a technical distinction we brought up in Chapter 9 - namely the difference between possibility and probability. We should also recall that an internally coherent interpretation is not necessarily coherent externally (you can have an idea that works in theory, but is not true in reality). So, as we examine the evidence, we must inquire about whether the interpretation is not only possible (theoretically), but whether it is plausible (likely).

We must ask whether there are alternative explanations, which account for all the facts in the claim, but also provide a different conclusion. If there are, then we must ask whether either option requires us to perform seemingly unnecessary mental gymnastics to make the facts fit that conclusion. If one explanation requires all sorts of additional interpretive tricks - like squinting at the data, or cherry-picking only specific data - while the other one does not, the least complex one is the more likely plausible one.

4. Can the claim be salvaged?

Finally, if the evidence is not good enough, or if the interpretation is less than plausible, we should ask whether the claim can still be salvaged? This step is not-so-necessary in pure analysis (more on that below), but it is a good idea in general. What we do as part of salvaging the claim is see whether any new data (which we may have independent of the claim being made), or different interpretation, etc. can make the claim functional. Just because the speaker screwed up, does not mean that we should throw away the whole claim. If introducing new data will let us make something functional of the claim, then that functional component is to our benefit – even if the speaker is only indirectly responsible for it. Their claim might be garbage, but we should see about recycling it.

In our baking example, this attempt to salvage a claim is something like trying to find alternative ingredients to make the recipe work. Maybe you don't have any sugar and can't buy any – meaning the cake is lost. Or, perhaps, you can substitute honey for sugar, and make it work. If you can, you still have a cake. Maybe not exactly as written in the recipe, but a cake nonetheless.

When we are doing pure analysis, we are not interested in making a claim work. Instead, we are evaluating someone else's claim "as-is." At that point, our job is not to salvage the claim. Pure analysis is the kind of thing we do when we are, for example, grading someone's math test. In such a case, our job is to see whether the answer is correct and (possibly) whether the process of solving the problem was correct; and then give them the grade for their results. We don't have to sit there and solve the problem ourselves or see what we can learn from the work they're showing.

Generally, pure analysis is reserved for certain kinds of academic work (like a professor grading a student's work). In these situations, we are not really engaging with the claim. Instead, we already know what's right and wrong (sometimes that is because we designed the question), and we're just processing the incoming information – like a scantron machine. Notice that this approach is completely different from any kind of conversation, debate, exploration of a topic, etc. While it is what may be academically required, or may be required in certain fields (like checking the load-calculations for an electric grid), it is not the kind of attitude that we should have in the vast majority of our interactions.

If you've ever watched any of the competitive cooking shows, this is the process that's used in judging the product that the competitors have made. The judges are not there to fix the problems the contestants made. Instead, they are there to judge the result "as-is," and decide whether they work or not; whether the contestants are staying or going home. On the other hand, when you're trying to make dinner, you're less interested in the exact specifications of the recipe, and more interested in getting a meal. Sure, the burger patty fell apart, but could you make Sloppy Joes out of it and avoid being hungry?

Since our interactions with claims are generally set up so that we learn something, this is not a "cooking show judge" position, it is a "make a meal" position. If you can salvage a bad idea, you and the other person get to eat. If not, the best you get is knowing what went wrong, so you don't do it again.

It bears noting that as we try to salvage the claim, we need to check our new implications to make sure they don't produce different sets of problems. A solution is not much of a solution if it simply exchanges one set of unsolvable problems for a different set of similarly unsolvable problems. If we think we have found a way to salvage the claim, we need to go back and start over at the conditional questions, and work our way through to the end of the *Claim Shredder Method* with the new claim.

Finalizing the Conclusion:

After all the analysis, we have to make a call as to whether the claim is good or not. At this point, we look at our results, and ask the following questions (the flowchart version makes the process easier):

1. Does this claim work as presented by the speaker (coherence, justification)?
    a. If it does, we move onto the evidence, to see if it bears out.
    b. If it does not, check if it can work with new limits.
        i. If it can't, then the claim is garbage.
        ii. If it can, check to see if the claim is functional within those new limits.
            1. If it is not functional, the claim is garbage.
            2. If it is functional, move onto the evidence, to see if it bears out.
2. Is the evidence sufficient to support the claim?
    a. If evidence is sufficient to support the claim, check whether this is the most plausible interpretation.
        i. If the claim is plausible, the claim is good.
        ii. If the claim is not plausible, the claim is possible, but unlikely (mostly garbage).
    b. If the evidence is not sufficient to support the claim, check to see if it can be salvaged.
        i. If it can't, the claim is garbage.
        ii. If it can be salvaged, the (new) claim is good.

Notice how quickly we can work our way through this last step - just yes/no answers. We can do so because we did all the heavy lifting in the previous steps. We assessed, analyzed, clarified, considered implications, etc. which then gave us the ability to answer these questions.

Notice also that our conclusion is, itself, a claim. Whether we conclude that the claim is valid or not, the *Claim Shredder Method* forces you to build a rational, fully supported justification of that conclusion, with a complete "paper trail" at every step. That paper trail can be easily checked by others, which means that the conclusion should have little or no wiggle room (if the process was done right).

This transparency of your own critical thinking method actually makes you a very good source for others to use, because all your work is clearly presented. As a consequence, I don't have to trust you, as a person, in order to trust your results - because your results are something that I can verify for myself.

CASE STUDY
QUESTIONS OF EVIDENCE

Turning back to our case study, we can now ask questions about the evidence for the claim.

What kind of evidence do we need?

Well, we can take a look back at our previous steps, and see every point of compromise we've run into.

1.   The speaker is iffy, non-expert, working for an organization that prioritizes "moving the markets," who has used click-bait/misleading headlines in the past, and whose stories rely on anonymous sources far too often for comfort.

2.   The audience is equally non-expert, reading a narrative without data, explicitly relying on the authoritative status of the speaker to make their decisions.

3.   The metrics are severely lacking in any kind of verifiable justification - asserting complete compromise of all security (including air-gaps), offering no proof, and relying on our trust in the authoritative source through information from anonymous sources.

4.   In clarifying the claim, we found a number of conditional points, which produce incoherent results.

We would need evidence enough to address all these issues, as well as answer additional questions about time travel and such, in order to make this claim work. Notice that, once written out together, the requirements for evidence add up to a very tall order, and paint a rather damning picture for the claim.

Let's consider what evidence we might find sufficient to deal with these points of compromise:

1.   If the speaker could provide us with the reason why he believes the story - what convinced him - then we could check whether that information is convincing to us. That means either information that we could verify, or sources of his information would have to be clearly revealed. If we have a "boy who cried wolf" problem, but he can also clearly show us the wolf in question, we can still believe him.

2.   There is nothing we can do about the audience. If they accept Bloomberg as an authoritative source, and do not demand that claims be justified to a higher standard, this is just a feature of the publication. Again, though, if we had a clear reason why the speaker accepted the truth of the claim and wrote it, then this problem could be made to vanish.

3.   A clear justification, with metrics, could convince us that there is a hidden chip, or that the chip can bypass air-gaps, etc.

4.   Additional information, clarification, details, etc. about various incoherent points could allow us to make sense of something like the time-travel issue. Maybe there is information that was not shared with us (and which we could not imagine at the time) that would make this apparent problem disappear.
For example, taking human life is prohibited in the Decalogue (10 Commandments), and yet we have examples of the death penalty being prescribed in the same text. It appears to be a contradiction. But we can make an argument that it is a prohibition on murder - not killing. Since the death penalty prescription is about punishment of some kind of evil (whether we agree that the issue is evil or not) there is a justification in the text for taking human life under those limited circumstances. This lets us solve the contradiction in two ways: 1) rule v exception, and 2) killing v murder.

In short, the evidence we need is the information for why the speaker believed the claim to begin with (or verifiable knowledge of who his sources are), the information needs to work, and the points of incoherence have to be resolved.

What kind of evidence do we have?

It turns out, we have no evidence for the claim. The entire claim is based solely on anonymous sources, which have provided us only with a story. There is no data, there is nothing we can go and verify for ourselves. So, we are left with only the option to blindly trust the claim, or not. To clarify, this is a case of blind trust, because we are entirely reliant on unknown people, their knowledge (which we can't verify), their good will in sharing the information (which we can't verify either), and the good will of the speaker (Jordan Robertson) in conveying the information to us.

In reality, Jordan Robertson could have invented the entire story, made up his sources, and we would have no way of distinguishing between the two stories. In both cases, trusting the story requires us to blindly believe his word. Additionally, I have no evidence that Jordan Robertson is so trustworthy that his word should override all the noted concerns.

Possibility v plausibility

Is the story possible? Maybe, if we squint hard enough. We would have to make all sorts of iffy assumptions (like Chinese government holding an annual ritual threatening of manufacturers), treason without reason, etc. to make this work.

Is the story plausible? Not even a little bit. Certain parts are definitely worth thinking about (at least if we turn them abstract enough). For example, the reliance on a supply chain that originates in a foreign country, and one known for trying to engage in corporate and government espionage, is a point we should worry about. However, the story as a whole is entirely implausible, even just as a story. If we were only taking it as seriously as a John Grisham novel, it would be a problem, because it is filled with plot holes.

Can the claim be salvaged?

Looking at the kinds of evidence needed for the claim, it seems rather dubious that we could salvage this claim. However, keep in mind that salvaging a claim does not require us to somehow salvage the original author or Bloomberg news. At this step we want to know whether the "China using a hardware hack through motherboards" issue might be real.

Unless you have access to some kind of information the rest of us don't know about, the answer is a hard no. Because the original claim is so outlandish (single chip bypasses all security), and because it lacks meaningful sources, we don't really have anywhere to start. That the Chinese government might do this if given a chance is nearly a certainty. However, because we don't have any indication that such a thing is possible (including according to verified experts), there is no decent starting point for data that might salvage the claim.

Finalizing our Conclusion

The claim certainly does not work "as-is," for reasons noted above. There is simply nothing approaching a coherent justification to support it. Sure, it sounds terrifying at first, but with a bit of digging, it turns out to be another click-bait headline, with no real substance.

Can we introduce new limits on the claim to make it work?

Given the nature of the claim, we can't. Even if we could exclude absolute levels of security compromise by the chip, there is no evidence at all for the existence of the chip. The best we could say is something like, "**If** the Chinese government did invent such a thing, and **if** they managed to get it onto motherboards, and **if** those motherboards were used by the noted companies, and **if** the unauthorized behavior of the computers went unnoticed, then we would have a problem." That's a lot of if's, with no justification to support any of them.

So, in two steps, we have come to the conclusion that the claim is garbage. Actually, it is so bad, on so many levels, that I can only describe it as a full-on dumpster fire.

All that work, from reading the article, to research, to finding out who Joe Grand is, took me about 2 hours to complete. And, I would like to note, I know nothing about the cybersecurity field. For someone with actual knowledge or expertise in the field, the time would be about 30-45 minutes. That's because they don't have to google every term and research every part of every claim - like I did.

Something to Keep in Mind

You might be thinking, *there is no way that actual experts fell for a claim like this!* The reality is, sadly, that in the weeks that it took the cybersecurity community to actually stop reacting (panic) about the claim, they had spent billions of dollars in man-hours on a problem that never existed. Additionally, Wall Street reacted so violently that Supermicro stock dropped just shy of 50% in the first 48 hours (it actually dropped by 60.5% for a bit on October 4th). It took 18 months for the stock price to return to levels before Jordan Robertson's claim. That means that not only the cybersecurity experts, but also the finance experts (among others) were fooled by the initial story - primarily because they did not respond rationally; they reacted emotionally. And that emotional reaction and panic lasted a good long while before some sense of rationality returned.

What it took Wall Street 18 months to figure out (so that the value of the stock returned to earlier levels), I figured out in 2 hours. That means that I had an 18 month head-start on the rest of Wall Street to invest into Supermicro. Why invest, you might be wondering? Because if the story is garbage (and it very clearly is), then there is no reason for Supermicro stock to have lost value. And because there was no reason for the loss of value, the value of the stock will return to normal. Since the value of the stock dropped by about 50%, that means that my money will double. Sure, I will have to wait a while for the rest of the stock market to figure out that the story is garbage, but they will eventually figure it out (because Supermicro is too big a company to simply fail).

In May 2021, Supermicro stock hit $40, up from the lowest price of $8.45 on October 4, 2018. Oh, and we never did find that chip on any motherboard.

The Claim Shredder Method, which is a philosophical critical thinking methodology, was applicable to both the cybersecurity and financial world; and it worked far more effectively than the tools and procedures of either of those fields. And on top of that, it did so in a tiny fraction of the time it took either of those fields to get it right, and with no secret sources of knowledge - just publicly available research.

Just as importantly, while the cybersecurity and financial world were reacting emotionally, the results of *The Claim Shredder Method* were not only rational, they were clear, transparent, and led to rock-solid conclusions, verifiable by anyone. Unlike cryptocurrency - which seems to rise and fall depending on what Elon Musk ate for breakfast today - this is not a guessing game. This is a matter of reason. It's no different than noticing that everyone else is freaking out because 2+2 = 7. You can easily figure out if they're right or wrong. The conclusion you rationally come to is that 2+2 = 4, and 4 ≠ 7, and so there is no reason to freak out. If you can gain additional benefits by responding rationally, instead of reacting emotionally, so much the better. Maybe it will give others an incentive to keep calm and think in the future.

All that's left at this point is to consider a common problem in this process (next chapter) and wrap it all up.

CHAPTER 19

LACK OF INFORMATION

Sooner or later, as we work with the *Claim Shredder Method* to engage with various claims, we will run into a problem: insufficient information available. What do we do when we encounter a claim for which there just is not enough available information? What do we do when there has not been enough time (or there are not enough records) to create a meaningfully contextual picture? This is a serious issue, because it leaves us unable to come to a conclusion about whether the claim is valid or otherwise. So, it would seem that the *Claim Shredder Method* fails us, right when we need it most.

For example, as we hear about something like a police shooting, we only have a tiny fraction of the available information available at the start. We might have the fact that the event has happened; we might have the identity of the police officer and of the deceased; we might even have some social media videos. But we are missing far more context than what we have. And yet, it is in the first hours of the story breaking that many people form their positions and attitudes - usually from sources pushing some kind of an agenda.

What do we mean by not enough information? Let's look at the kind of language often used in these kinds of stories: in order for police use of force (in this case, deadly force) to be a "problem," it needs to be *disproportionate to the context of the situation*. We certainly think that a police officer using deadly force to stop a murderous maniac shooting at random people is legitimate. No one complained that the police should have used less force trying to deal with the Las Vegas Shooter. We don't find that the same use of force is legitimate if the person shot was walking around handing out flowers. If we don't know the context (because we can't know the context yet, because the information has not yet been released), then we can't come to a conclusion about whether the force was disproportionate or not. Until we know what was going on, we can't know whether we agree or disagree with the use of force.

Fortunately for us, the *Claim Shredder Method* still works. True, the final conclusion can't be reached right away, but that issue will generally resolve itself with a bit of time - as more information becomes available. What we can do - and should do - is all the prepwork: research, analysis, terms, definitions, etc. But then, following the *wu-wei* approach, we have to sit back and allow the story to unfold. As it does, new information will fill in the last pieces of the context for us. We will get to the details of this process in a moment.

But don't we want to know the truth as soon as events happen? Of course we do. However, as with the case of the dumbbell or the manager title, we have to get the rest of the information first. Sure, we have the title, but we need to see the performance to know whether the title fits the reality. Since none of us are operating with omniscience, we have to get enough meaningful information to come to the final conclusion. The *Claim Shredder Method* still gives us the most functional way to do that, but it does not magically create information out of thin air.

So, what do we do when we don't have enough information?

The first thing is to recognize when information is likely to be missing, and what parts of the claim (story) hinge on that missing information. That tells us where our critical points will be. In our example above, we can't decide whether the use of force was justified, because we don't know whether it was proportionate. So now we know that the justified/unjustified part of the claim hinges on the proportionality, and that depends on the context of the event (what happened that led up to the use of force?) for which we have to wait to get the full picture.

The second thing to do is to get all the information we can get, and be extra careful about the sources of that information. If you will recall Chapter 5, the various authoritative sources are likely to be pushing a whole host of possible agendas, experts will be giving their opinions, etc. We don't want to simply accept information blindly, and without validation. We certainly don't want to rely on anonymous sources that come without proof.

Third, we run through the entire *Claim Shredder Method*, but with some changes:

1. If we have two competing stories (or more), we have to actually deal with all the stories at the same time.

   a. Make a list, and run through each story, one at a time.

2. We need to identify the key premises used in the justifications (metrics), because those ideas are what the whole claim will hinge upon.

   a. For example, the idea of "proportionate response" is not a matter of personal preference, public opinion, etc. It is a legally defined term, and specifically defined for police departments by the individual states. That means that you have to check the definition of that metric before you can meaningfully understand the claim.

      i. If we find that different claims are using the terminology differently, then they are not actually talking about the same thing, it only sounds like they are (think back to the Dawkins/Rev. Hall example).

      ii. If one claim is about whether the police officer acted disproportionately, the claim is relying on legal definitions and state policies. If the other claim is about whether such a use of force should be legal (whether we should change the laws and practices that govern policing), then the claim is relying on moral judgments and practical considerations for effective policing.

      iii. Notice that the two sides might not be talking about the same issue. The use of force may be proportionate and legally defensible, and also morally bad and in need of legal revision. As a result, it is possible for both claims to be right or wrong, at the same time - since they're not arguing about the same thing. If the two claims are not talking about the same issue, then they are not competing with each other; they are talking about entirely different things. If you like, you can go and work on them individually, but you must remember that if one is true, that does not make the other one false, or vice versa.

3. When we get to the claim working "as-is" and evidence, we use the key premises to create conditionally functional conclusions for each competing claim.

   a. A conditionally functional conclusion is a conditional statement (if-then), that gives us the answer to the question of validity of the claim, and under what conditions the claim will be valid (for each story).

   b. This process is very similar to considering implications for what must be true or false, except that the known and unknown features are flipped. Ordinarily, we put the part we know as the condition (the "if" part of the statement), and then look for what else would be true or false (the "then" part of the statement). With conditionally functional conclusions, we are trying to determine which conditions we need to make the claim true, so the "if" part of the statement is the key features of the claim, which we are not yet sure are true or not. The "then" part is the claim itself.

   c. For example, after we have looked up all the terms and definitions, then we can say something like, *If it is true that X, and Y, and Z, then the context of the event was such that **the shooting was not a proportionate response*** (notice that the claim comes as the consequence of the key features being true).

4. Then, we have to sit back and wait for additional information to come to light. When we get the additional information, we then go on to compare it with our conditionally functional conclusions. At that point, the new information is likely to be favoring one side over the other - and we revise our conditionally functional conclusions to reflect the new information. Then we wait again.

a. For example, you might find out that X is true. Now the revised contextually functional conclusion would be changed to, *If it is true that Y and Z, then the context was such that the shooting was not a proportionate response* (notice that we omitted the X this time, because it has already been confirmed as true).

b. Updating conditional functionality may require us to add new problems for a claim to solve. A point in favor of claim A may be a point against claim B. Just as we had to ask for additional evidence to account for a point of compromise in the *Claim Shredder* conclusions, we now have to present a justification and provide evidence for how claim B could be true, if the new information presents a problem for it.

5. At some point, the new information will fall in favor of one claim, and create impossible evidence requirements for other possible claims, leaving us with the most plausible conclusion.

So, let's consider the police shooting case here. When the news breaks, all we have is the statement that a police officer(s) shot and killed some person P. That is not, in itself, a piece of information we can meaningfully interpret yet. We need to know who, we need to know why, and we need to know about the events that led up to the issue (context). This is the minimum information we need.

News source A tells us that this was a legitimate and justified use of force. News source B tells us that this was not a legitimate or justified use of force. We have video of the incident, but it was filmed once the incident was already in progress, so we can't tell with certainty what actually happened. Also, the video is presented by someone, and we don't know if they're showing the whole thing or if they decided to use creative editing.

What do we do?

1. Consider both claims simultaneously.

a. In this case, we only have two options - the officer was justified in the use of force, or was not.

2. Identify the key premises (metrics) of each claim

a. What is the key premise in claim A? Look up terms, definitions, etc.

b. What is the key premise in claim B? Look up terms, definitions, etc

3. Check to make sure that the claims are talking about the same thing. If they are not, then there is no comparison possible. You can examine each claim individually, but not in comparison.

4. Create conditionally functional conclusions for each claim and write them out.

   a. Write out your conclusions as follows:

      i. *If it is true that [X and Y and Z], then claim A is true.*

      ii. *If it is true that [1 and 2 and 3], then claim B is true.*

5. Watch for new information, update the conditionally functional conclusions, and note ways in which we may have to account for the new information in other claims. Let's say that it turns out that Z is true. Now the updated conditionally functional conclusions might look like this:

   a. *If it is true that [X and Y], then A is true.*

   b. *If it is true that [1 and 2 and 3, **and we can account for Z being true**], then claim B is true.*

6. At a certain point, the ambiguity is going to clarify into a meaningful answer - the police officer cannot both be acting in accordance with the rules and not acting in accordance with the rules. For example, if body-cam footage is released where the person shot is charging at the police officer, waiving a gun around and screaming bloody murder, then the use of deadly force is justified - and you can't come up with a way that will make it unjustified. And then you have your conclusion.

Notice that we can do almost all the work here in advance. We check the speaker, the audience, the available metrics, we clarify each position, we ask conditional questions (which help us to create conditionally functional conclusions). And then, we don't make a decision of what is or is not true. Instead, we wait until we get information that will lead us in the correct direction by filling in the rest of the content.

This way, we are engaged in both *zhengming* and *wu-wei*. We have defined the terms, and now we're waiting for the situation to show us what the truth is. Our job becomes something like waiting for sufficient information to pass judgment. But we must wait, or else we're not letting the information tell us what is true. Instead, we are letting our emotions make assumptions and "feel" their way to the conclusion.

Imagine what that would look like in a courtroom: the defendant is brought in, and the jury decides whether they're guilty or not before they have heard the evidence. The need to avoid this kind of lynch-mob mentality is why we have the requirement for an "impartial jury" as part of the 6th Amendment to the Constitution.[62]

Since we're already on the topic of police shootings, we can use it to point out some good general rules on the kinds of stories that tend to push a lot of emotional buttons.

Something to consider is that it generally takes several days (if not weeks) for certain tasks to be accomplished, before we can have a meaningful amount of information to really be able to pass judgment. Things like autopsy and an autopsy report, bodycam footage, the police department going through information to try to figure out what happened (and whether officers' statements match the information they have), etc. all take time to complete. And keep in mind that the police department can't just stop dealing with a million other things it constantly does (like having to respond to 911 calls, dealing with crime, and continuing other ongoing investigations). So, giving ourselves that time to get reliable information, as well as a reliable quantity of information and context, is a far safer bet than picking a side. By the way, it does not matter which side you pick here. Neither side has any actual idea about what happened, so any "picking sides" requires us to act blindly, with no information and no context. I would advise waiting at least 3 days (72 hours) before passing any kind of judgment, although you can start working on it as soon as you have any information.

Another thing to consider is that "common sense" ideas about the police and laws are rarely true (this works across nearly all issues in all fields). It's one thing to morally disagree with certain behaviors, laws, policies, etc. It is an entirely different thing to classify them as "criminal." Criminality hinges on there being a law against that specific act - or that class of behaviors. For example, it is not illegal for a police officer to use deadly force if they feel threatened. It is illegal for me (a civilian) to do the same against an officer if I feel threatened. Whether I like the laws or not, the question of whether the officer did something legally wrong or not is not about my feelings or yours, it is about the laws and policies in place. A good first step to making sure the claim works here is to check the text of the laws, and the available interpretation by the courts. That way, you might at least be able to salvage a bad claim. A decent place to see some of these ideas explored can be found in an entertaining and educational form at Nate the Law-

---

62   https://constitution.congress.gov/constitution/amendment-6/

yer[63] or <u>Legal Eagle</u>.[64]

Notice that the exact same idea is true if we're talking about medicine, law, politics, business, education, etc. There are specific rules, procedures, laws, and a million other things that we - as members of the general public - have no clue about. That means that having a coherent opinion requires us to go educate ourselves on these issues first and to get the context, otherwise we are just making face noises while pretending to have a position. The waiting process to get information is also true in every other field as well. It simply takes time for information to be sorted and come out. Picking your position before you have sufficient information is always about blind following - which is both emotional and contradictory to critical thinking.

We are frequently placed in situations where we are missing information. While the *Claim Shredder Method* cannot magically give you the answers, what it can do is get you as close as possible with the available information, and tell you what new information to look out for, because specific information will tilt the scales this way or that. Additionally, the *Claim Shredder Method* also tells us what information we need, even if we don't have it.

Sometimes the reason why the information does not seem to be available is because we don't know that we need to look for it. This can be a case of ignorance by ignorance or ignorance by relevance, and this is the reason why this book is focused on knowing what questions to ask. With the *Claim Shredder* drawing our attention to the right kinds of information we need, the context problem can get resolved. Once you know what you're looking for it's much easier to find and recognize it.

It is important to know what we do and do not know, and it is critical to be able to step back and say, "I don't know," when the issue is something that we have not thoroughly examined or something on which the data is still not available. And here, we come full circle to the emotional, reactive attitudes, as opposed to the rational, responsive ones.

We don't like to admit our ignorance, not even to ourselves. How many times have you jumped

---

63   Search "Nate the Lawyer" on YouTube, or go to https://www.youtube.com/channel/UCD5_QIM67BZJdh9AwZ-v3soA

64   Search "Legal Eagle" on YouTube, or go to https://www.youtube.com/channel/UCpa-Zb0ZcQjTCPP1Dx_1M8Q

into a conversation to offer an opinion, knowing full-well that you have no idea what you're talking about? How many times have you realized that you have no clue what you're actually talking about in the middle of a discussion? And when you realized that, how many times did you actually stop and say that you don't know? How many times did you just continue having an emotional spasm? This is part of our ego, we are embarrassed by ignorance, and so we don't want to admit it. If you don't have all the details of an issue, that is a fixable problem.

We are all "stupid." Whenever I don't know about some field, some issue, some problem, I am stupid with respect to that specific thing. Since no one knows everything, we are all stupid about a lot of different things. That's fine. We can overcome our stupidity by asking questions, paying attention, learning, and asking more questions to make sure our understanding of the issue is solid. Suddenly, we become less stupid.

The problem is when we don't recognize, or don't want to admit, that we are stupid. You've all heard the phrase, "the first step to solving a problem is admitting that you have a problem." But if your emotions keep you from recognizing that you have a problem, then you get stuck. Not only are you stupid, you are also not able become less stupid.

This was part of Al-Ghazali's point in Chapter 2: if we do not clearly understand an idea, we should not be in a rush to offer an opinion on it. Unless we understand what is going on, our opinions make no sense - because we literally don't know what we are talking about. While we don't have to go and get a Ph.D. in the field, we are all capable of getting informed on the issue, and then using the *Claim Shredder* to check whether the claim works or not.

Pop quiz: did you respond or react to the example of police shootings? Did you read carefully, or did you start thinking of counterarguments before you finished the section? Were you cheering for the argument or against it - or did you sit back to see where it was headed?

It is my hope that you have all become better critical thinkers, and that the content of this book will serve you in your academic, professional, and personal lives. At the very least, if we are asking questions and trying to understand, we are all less likely to to turn into screaming, murderous mobs, and that's at least a step in the right direction.

CHAPTER 20

THE CLAIM SHREDDER METHOD

At this point, it should be fairly obvious that the Claim Shredder is a streamlined and organized way of applying context, in order to perform critical thinking and critical analysis. At the end of the process, we have an idea of whether the claim itself is valid or not, and why. Additionally, we also have the tools to demonstrate our conclusions to any audience, of any technical skill. While the Claim Shredder can be tweaked for any field of interest, it is ultimately a tool of reason – and requires nothing more than reason to make it work and to make it understood.

Though the name is a bit aggressive, the *Claim Shredder Method* is actually not geared towards proving or disproving claims. It is geared towards a careful and holistic analysis of claims and their functionality. The conclusions (valid/garbage) are a mere side-effect. If you approach the system in this way, then the entire "combative attitude," which leads to reactions (yours and everyone else's) drops away. You're merely getting all the information in order, inquiring about meaning, and actually trying to make it work as best you can. This is often reciprocated by the other party, and it ends up being a collaborative effort at finding the validity and functionality of a claim.

In this collaborative approach, the *Claim Shredder Method* is trying to emulate the P4C (philosophy for children) methodology. While the combative approach leads to people picking sides and trying to "win" at all costs (we've all been in the middle of an argument when we realize we're in the wrong and kept going anyway), the collaborative method has a very different feel to it.

In my own practice, I have watched a group of 10-year-olds come up with answers they were positive about, then reconsider, backtrack, find the problems, and amend their position – all on their own, and with no input from me (other than an occasional question). That's because no one was trying to win, they were just trying to solve the problem. Similarly, I have watched any number of college students present their case (with help from the rest of the class), only to stop 10 minutes in, and declare that the position is actually broken, and then clarify where they think the break happens. This is because their audience (the class and myself) are not arguing against them, but are working with them to clarify the idea – even when I know in advance that it will fail miserably.

Finally, the Claim Shredder has an additional function. As someone now aware of the system, your own arguments and writing should always integrate the questions, or answers to those questions, into your own claims. In that way, your position comes across much stronger – and rightly so! You have already considered the kinds of challenges you are likely to face from a discerning audience and have preempted the questions with a clear set of answers. But, if you cannot satisfactorily answer these questions yourself, as the originator of the claim, the claim is weak and should be rethought or abandoned.

In the following section, we will recap the system in short, through a simple template, with graphics – to make your own use of the system quicker and easier.

The CLAIM SHREDDER Method

Welcome to the Claim Shredder Method,

To make your transition to the Claim Shredder Method style of critical thinking smoother, this document will provide you with a general template to follow in your analysis.

The core benefit is that the Claim Shredder is particularly interested in making sure that your analysis is properly justified – which can make your life significantly easier in communicating why a claim should be taken seriously or dismissed. By providing a solid justification up front, you can avoid needless secondary issues and conflicting assessments.

Your goal in using this template should be to advance to the point of not needing to use it. After several analyses, you should be able to complete the process using only the Claim Shredder flowchart. After a dozen analyses, you should internalize this process completely. That said, the template and the flowchart provide you with a nice set of reference points, especially as you communicate with other members of your and other teams. It allows everyone to get on the same page, regardless of how early or late they get in on the action.

As with all analysis tools that aim at clarity and nuance, the kinds of questions you will need to ask, and the kinds of issues you will need to consider, cannot be fully noted ahead of time. Each claim has its own context, its own peculiarities, and you may need to ask additional questions, or disregard some of the ones noted here. The Claim Shredder Method is designed to allow you to do just that, and thus to customize the specific variables to match your own needs. The only thing to note is that customization should make sure that the kinds of questions you are adding go in the correct area, and that the removal of a question will not compromise your analysis capabilities. A simple way of doing the latter is to ask whether the inclusion/exclusion of the question gives you any meaningful information - or whether it results in losing meaningful information.

The following template is split up into two general sections: argument build up and decision. Argument Build up is composed of three general questions: Speaker, Audience, and Method (metrics). Decision is composed of Method (interpretation) and is affected by the results of the argument build up.

The CLAIM SHREDDER Method

PHASE 1 - ARGUMENT BUILDUP

PHASE 2 - DECISION

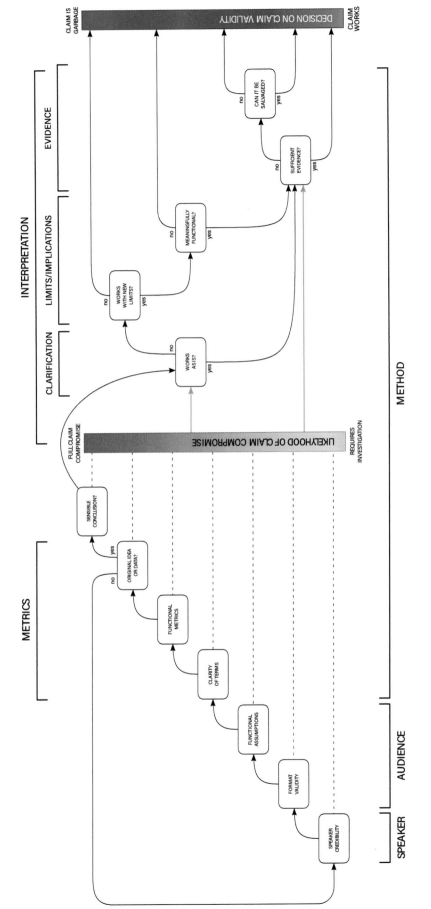

SPEAKER
- Speaker qualifications?
- Speaker affiliations?
- Speaker history?
- Is this a sales pitch?
- Speaker intent?

AUDIENCE
- Who is the intended recipient?
- Explain nuance in phrasing
- Clarify speaker intent
- Formatting and data type?
- Implicit assumptions?

METHOD

METRICS
- What is being measured?
- How is it being measured?
- Are terms and definitions clear?

BEWARE: statistics games

All data is biased, there are infinite possible interpretations.
▶ Focus on FUNCTIONALITY

INTERPRETATION
- Clarify the claim
- Check implications and limits
- Evaluate the evidence
- Is a more functional interpretation available?
- If broken, can the claim be salvaged?

READING THE FLOWCHART

The flowchart represents the entirety of the Claim Shredder Method. It is divided up into two phases.

Phase 1 is the Argument Build Up, which is the critical thinking portion. It's about dissecting the claim, seeing all the moving parts, and having a sense of what's going right or wrong.

1. As you ask the context questions, if the answer is positive, you move up to the next question.

2. If the answer negative, **note the level of claim compromise** (orange-red bar in the middle), and then move up to the next question.

   o The higher you go, the worse a negative answer compromises the claim.

Phase 2 is the Decision phase, which is all about critical analysis. The argument buildup gives you the tools to use in making your decision, and all those compromise points play a role in our decision on the functionality and evidence of the conclusion. That's why we note all those claim compromise points: because they have a lot of bearing on the question whether the claim works as is, and whether the evidence is sufficient.

- Notice that this section is a clear-cut yes/no reading of the options.

- Only the **"Works as is?"** and the **"Sufficient Evidence?"** questions are about direct interpretation of the claim.

- The rest of the questions are attempts to salvage varieties of claim failures.

- The conclusions fall on a spectrum from **Valid** to **Garbage**. The designations and the relative claim conclusions on the flowchart are there to give you a general sense of the most likely threat level resulting from each option. There are plenty of outliers in both directions, though things that come up on either extreme end of the scale do not generally change.

Along the bottom of the flowchart, you will find the cheat-sheet of the major questions for each of the three main context points.

PHASE 1 - ARGUMENT BUILDUP

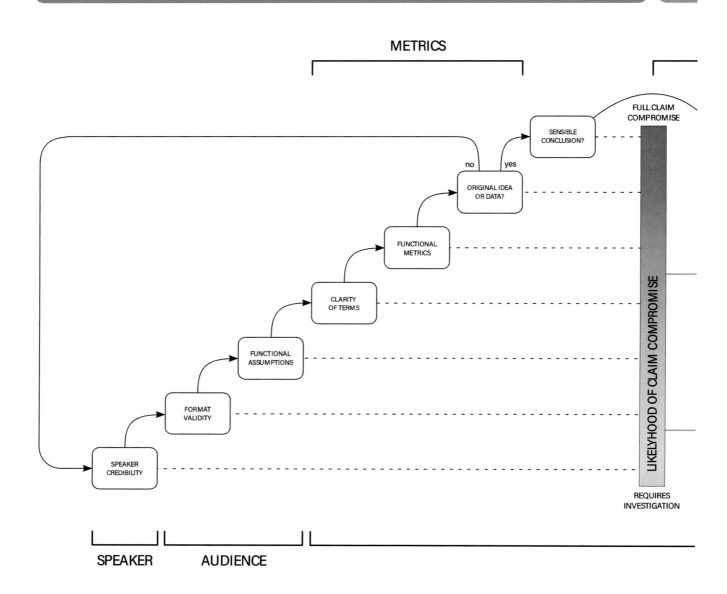

PHASE 1 - ARGUMENT BUILDUP

SPEAKER / AUDIENCE / METHOD: METRICS

S PEAKER (Who is the speaker, author, source of claim?)

- Name of person(s)?

- Are they an expert?

    o Are they an expert in this specific field?

    o What are their qualifications?

    o What proof do you have?

- Who is the employer (includes self-employment)?

    o What is the nature of the employer? (Think-tank, non-profit, vendor, etc.)

    o Do they have a vested interest in any particular interpretation?

- What is the history of the speaker/employer on:

    o Making similar claims?

    o Being correct/incorrect on such claims?

- Is the claim a sales pitch? (direct or indirect)

- What seems to be the intent of the speaker?

SPEAKER / AUDIENCE / METHOD: METRICS

AUDIENCE (Who is the intended recipient of the communication?)

- Who is the intended recipient of the communication?

    o How do you know? (commonly by source publication and their audience)

- What is the formatting?

    o Is it a narrative?

    o Is it technical, detailed, structured, etc.?

- What is the data type? (there is the option of "none")

    o Numbers or percentages?

    o Time frames?

    o Comparisons of X to Y? (could be by time, by number, etc.)

- What are the implicit assumptions of the audience?

    o What beliefs does the **intended** audience already have?

    o What assumptions, biases, etc. are built into those beliefs?

SPEAKER / AUDIENCE / METHOD: METRICS

METHOD: METRICS (What is being measured/considered and how?)

- What is being measured/considered/claimed?

    o If not explicitly stated, state it yourself.

- How is it being measured/considered/claimed?

    o What is the exact system of measurement/consideration/justification?

    o Where is the data coming from?

        · If original, what are the details of collection?

        · If not original, who is the source? (and go check the source)

    o How is the data supposed to be related to the object being measured?

        · Is this **functional**?

- What terms are being used?

    o How are those terms defined?

    o Are the definitions industry standard?

        · If not, what is the difference between the two?

        · If not, is the claim definition **functional** for your purposes?

Sensible Conclusion? (Does this seem to make sense?)

At the end of the argument build up process, you should take a moment to review the information you have assembled so far. Then look at the conclusion of the claim.

Does the conclusion seem sensible, in light of the argument build up?

Think of this as a smell-test. As you run through several of these analyses, you should begin to develop this sense of "something wrong" with the claim. If you pay attention to it, you will begin to pick up on how this sense tends to reflect in what is generally wrong with the claim. This will allow you to zero-in on the particular kinds of failures quicker.

PHASE 1 - ARGUMENT BUILDUP

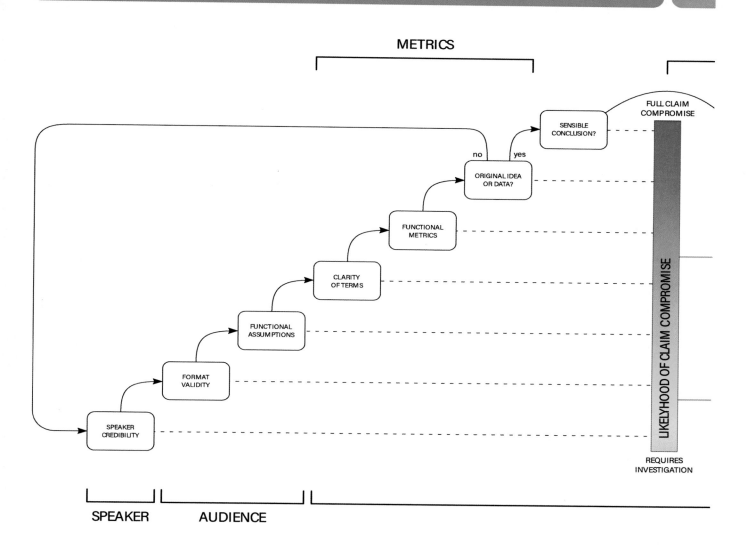

PHASE 2 - DECISION

INTERPRETATION

CLARIFICATION   LIMITS/IMPLICATIONS   EVIDENCE

FULL CLAIM
COMPROMISE

CLAIM IS
GARBAGE

LIKELYHOOD OF CLAIM COMPROMISE

no

WORKS
WITH NEW
LIMITS?

yes

no

WORKS
AS IS?

yes

no

MEANINGFULLY
FUNCTIONAL?

yes

no

CAN IT BE
SALVAGED?

yes

no

SUFFICIENT
EVIDENCE?

yes

DECISION ON CLAIM VALIDITY

REQUIRES
INVESTIGATION

CLAIM
WORKS

METHOD

METHOD: INTERPRETATION

CLARIFICATION: (The Claim in light of the conclusion and our research so far)

- Answers must account for noted points of claim compromise as far as possible

- What do you mean by that?

    - What does that claim (conclusion) mean?

    - Clarify terminology, definitions (commit to a concrete, non-vague phrasing of the claim)

- Can you say that in a different way?

    - You can't rephrase vague/poorly defined ideas – because they are not understood.

- Can you give an example?

    - If there is no example, what exactly is the point?

- Why do you believe that?

    - What is the justification for the claim?

    - Is it original, or taken from a different source?

    - If from a different source, is that source **functional?**

METHOD: INTERPRETATION

Conditionals: (If-Then statements, with Implications and Limits)

- Answers must account for noted points of claim compromise as far as possible

- Is there a case where it's not true?

    o If so, under what limits does the claim still work?

- If the claim is true, what else must be true?

    o What are the positive implications of accepting the claim?

        ▪ NOTE: These implications introduce secondary implications (implications from the implications) and limits.

    o Does the claim work **functionally** under the new implications and limits?

- If the claim is true, what cannot be true?

    o What are the negative implications of accepting the claim?

        ▪ NOTE: These implications introduce secondary implications (implications from the implications) and limits.

    o Does the claim work **functionally** under the new implications and limits?

METHOD: INTERPRETATION

EVIDENCE: - Answers must account for noted points of claim compromise as far as possible

- What kind of evidence is necessary?

    o   Accounting for the claim, and the problems posed by the levels of compromise

    o   Do this step first, to avoid inserting your own bias into understanding evidence

- What kind of evidence is available?

    o   How does the available evidence stack up against the necessary evidence?

    o   Does the evidence point to the claim being possible or probable?

    o   Is there a more functional interpretation of the evidence possible?

        ▪   If so, does how does that strengthen or weaken the claim?

- Is this interpretation the most plausible one?

    o   Is it internally coherent?

    o   Is it externally coherent?

- If evidence is lacking, is there a way to salvage the claim with new data?

Made in the USA
Monee, IL
18 December 2023

49934827R00133